IN PURSUIT OF THE MIRACULOUS

IN PURSUIT OF THE MIRACULOUS

Why We Should Expect Miracles Today

Roy Todd

MILTON KEYNES • COLORADO SPRINGS • HYDERABAD

15 14 13 12 11 10 09   7 6 5 4 3 2 1

This edition published 2009 by Authentic Media
9 Holdom Avenue, Bletchley, Milton Keynes, MK1 1QR, UK
1820 Jet Stream Drive, Colorado Springs, CO 80921, USA
Medchal Road, Jeedimetla Village, Secunderabad 500 055, A.P., India
www.authenticmedia.co.uk

Authentic Media is a division of Biblica UK, previously IBS-STL UK. Biblica UK is limited by guarantee, with its registered office at Kingstown Broadway, Carlisle, Cumbria, CA3 0HA. Registered in England & Wales No. 1216232. Registered charity in England & Wales No. 270162 and Scotland No. SCO40064.

British Library Cataloguing in Publication Data
A catalogue record for this book is available from the British Library
ISBN-13: 978-1-86024-772-9

Cover Design by fourninezero design.
Print Management by Adare
Printed in Great Britain by J. F. Print, Sparkford, Somerset

This book is dedicated to the many church leaders who've believed in my calling enough to give me opportuntities to minister. I'll never forget that.

CONTENTS

FOREWORD

In the past ten years, my family has encountered some pretty big mountains. My wife had major back problems. Then my son had to face the challenge of cancer at just 16 years of age. Yet through it all, I believe more today in the miraculous power of Jesus than ever before. In the midst of life's complexities, with its challenges and disappointments, I would rather listen to a man who is heavily leaning on God than an 'expert' who has it all theoretically worked out. That's why I love this book.

The very title *In Pursuit of the Miraculous* instantly captures the honesty and integrity of Roy Todd. He's not portraying himself as someone with a formula in place to bring instant success. Rather, this is as a man who is on a constant quest and an exciting adventure of faith. I get the feeling that the desire for the miraculous is so strong that Roy is willing to be misunderstood or to make mistakes rather than merely opt for mediocrity and back off from challenges.

The book is interlaced with personal stories which give it credibility, since the author is clearly speaking from personal experience. Yet with honesty and compassion, he shares the struggles as well as the breakthroughs. It's great to hear that the man who now speaks and ministers to thousands of people started from small beginnings. This helps me as a reader – hearing his inward thoughts and sometimes of his lack of feelings, too, as he prays for the sick. This is not a story written to make Roy Todd look good. It's a book that honours Jesus.

I also love the way that God's word is always emphasized as the basis for action. Stepping out on this solid ground puts Roy in the line of many great people who have seen a release of God's power in the past. But more than that, Roy is pressing forward, believing that there is far more ahead – inspiring us, his readers, to pursue the same.

Another essential element for the pursuit that Roy emphasizes is the importance of character. As I have had the privilege of getting to know Roy over the past few years, I can see that this is something which he personally displays. I have a number of 'miracle' books sitting on my bookshelf. They often seem so easy – even a bit unreal. But *In Pursuit of the Miraculous* is written from a basis of integrity – from a man who inspires faith and hope whilst not being unreal.

I know that Roy is a man still very much 'in pursuit'. In fact, he's getting more and more breakthroughs on his journey. I want to encourage him in these words to press harder and to go for the impossible. Our nation needs people who carry this anointing and our world desperately needs this kind of ministry. Be inspired.

Stuart Bell, Senior Minister, New Life Church, Lincoln and leader of the Ground Level network

INTRODUCTION

One dictionary definition of miracles is that they are 'remarkable and welcome events that seem impossible to explain'.

But can they still happen today? Should we expect them? Jesus certainly encouraged his disciples to anticipate miraculous accompaniments to their proclamation of his good news. In Mark 16:17–18 he emphasizes five signs that 'will accompany those who believe' (v17). While it's unlikely that this list is exhaustive, it does indicate the types of miraculous signs that could be expected:

Casting out demons – signs of God's **P**ower
Speaking in new tongues – signs of God's **P**resence
Picking up snakes – signs of God's **P**rotection
Drinking deadly poison and not being harmed – signs of God's **P**reservation
Placing hands on sick people so they can recover – signs of God's **P**rovision

So if we accept that miracles do happen today, how might we see more of the miraculous in the twenty-first century? How can they be experienced? Just what kind of faith is needed for them to happen? Are there hindrances that can stop them occurring and if so, what are they? Perhaps you need a personal miracle. Maybe it's a desire to help someone else receive one. You might even be longing for both.

Well, I want to help you on your journey. You see, I'm absolutely convinced that miracles still happen today. Nothing is impossible with God. He can minister to anyone whose heart is open. Moving in the realm of the miraculous is not a specialist calling reserved for only a few big shots. Such thinking is completely contrary to the reason why the Holy Spirit came: to empower *all* of God's people. Surely the time has well and truly come for the body of Christ to rise up in the authority that is already available to us.

This book is an expression of my heart to share some principles with you that I have learned during my own pursuit of the miraculous over the past decade. Through it, I want you to be better equipped to experience all that God has for you. It doesn't claim to be a quick guide to all the answers you've ever sought, as it would be unreal of me to present it like that. Besides, I've never felt comfortable reading 'how to' books – they often show little or no understanding of the diversity of people's circumstances and needs. The main ingredient I've put into this book is reality mixed with a large dose of faith. By sharing from my own ponderings and wonderings, I want to inspire you to see more of the miraculous in and through your own life.

So if you find anything I've written so far resonates with you, I challenge you to read on. As you do, allow your heart to be stirred to new levels of trust in a God who can do 'immeasurably more than all we ask or imagine, according to his power that is at work within us' (Eph. 3:20). With greater conviction and passion than we've ever had before, together let's experience God's power so we can be channels through which his miraculous glory is manifested.

1

A TALE OF THE UNEXPECTED

Sometimes in life, things happen unexpectedly. You plan, prepare and process your way through the options, and just when you think you've got it all worked out, something comes along that's completely out of the blue and totally disrupts your programme.

You see, on my journey of faith, I've discovered something about God. He's not predictable, because he's always a step ahead of where you are. It really is a mistake to try to second-guess him. Logic doesn't always figure in his way of doing things either, at least as far as human logic is concerned. He can't be outsmarted or outwitted, as he has a distinct advantage – he already knows what's ahead. His vantage point is high enough to view what's around each bend of life. In fact, he's the one who created the corner in the first place. And by the way, he created life too.

The truth is that there's nothing impossible with him. No one can be compared with him. He's all-seeing, all-knowing and all-present. That's what makes him who he is. He's God. And it's because he is who he is that I believe miracles still happen, even today.

Unexpected

My own adventure into the miraculous certainly wasn't planned intentionally by me. In fact it amazes me that I find myself writing a book on the subject. But I guess that's God for you – full of surprises.

It's not that there was a time in my life when I didn't believe in miracles. The truth is that I've always believed in them. Brought up in a Spirit-filled church in Belfast where faith was strong and the Bible taken seriously, I really had no choice but to. Yet when I started out as an evangelist, I never thought they would play a major part in my ministry. I'm a communicator, so I always felt God would merely use my preaching to draw people to personal faith. Actually, I really wanted to be like my hero, Billy Graham. Miracles were never a feature of his ministry, yet millions of people became Christians at his meetings. But God had other ideas for me. Have you ever noticed that he often takes you in the direction you least expect?

Little did I realize then that signs and wonders would become a huge accompaniment to my ministry. I still don't quite understand why I should be the kind of person who moves in the miraculous. I certainly don't fit the role of the glammed-up preacher who dramatically announces each miracle like a game show host to the applause of a hysterical audience. I'm just a normal bloke, born and raised in Northern Ireland during the height of the Troubles.

My Journey

'So when did you begin to see miracles happen in your ministry?' That's a question I'm often asked. Sometimes people anticipate a breathtaking answer involving incredible stories of Shekinah glory, Isaiah-like God encounters, life-after-death experiences, angelic visitations and the rest. But looking back, the first major miracle I ever witnessed involved none of those things. As a wet behind the ears 21-year-old evangelist, I usually preached to small congregations with as few as ten people and rarely more than fifty. So you can imagine my reaction when one day I received an invitation to be the guest speaker at an event in the north-east of England at which 300 people would gather. I gladly accepted, and prepared a brand-new sermon especially for the occasion (I had three usable sermons up to that point). I even rehearsed it a number of times in front of a mirror so I would get it just right on the night.

After weeks of waiting, the day of the big meeting finally came. I drove to the venue feeling excited and nervous at the same time. However, when I arrived and saw a packed car park, nervousness became my predominant emotion: I was now on the verge of facing the largest congregation I'd ever addressed. But I had no idea that this meeting would take an unexpected twist – one that would literally change the course of my ministry.

At 7 p.m. the service began. It began optimistically enough, but after the first few songs it started to drag. The format was roughly this: three fast songs followed by three slow songs, then another fast song (for the offering – cheerful giving and all that), followed by some slow songs, some slower songs and then the slowest songs. At this point, it was as if the meeting became transfixed in a state of slow motion, and I desperately wanted to press a fast-forward button to speed the proceedings up. The worship time just went on and on, and then when it looked as though it might finish it went on again. Meanwhile, I felt concerned in case people got bored and left early, thus missing the wonderful new sermon I'd prepared especially for them. After all, the reason why they'd come was to hear me preach, right? Well, that's what I thought.

By around 9 p.m., the elderly pastor leading the service eventually stood up on the platform to introduce me. In his strong north-eastern accent he said, 'We have a young man as our guest speaker this evening. His name is, ah, oh . . .' Then he stopped, looked at me from the platform and publicly asked, 'What's your name, son?' In a James Bond-esque moment, I made my dramatic introduction, announcing, 'My name's Todd: Roy Todd.' However, the poignancy of the moment was completely lost as the minister put his hand to his ear, positioned it like a satellite dish towards me and said, 'Speak up, son, I can't hear you.' This time, I confirmed my identity in less dramatic manner, simply replying 'Roy Todd' in a slightly louder voice.

'Ah, yes,' he said. 'We have a young man called Roy Todd. He has come all the way from Ireland especially to speak to us tonight.' (I'd actually been resident in England for three years at that point.) 'Let's give him a very special welcome as he comes to the platform.'

As I approached the stage, the welcome of the 300-strong congregation was underwhelming to say the least, as only about three of them joined in the applause. I felt somewhat deflated, as I could never have imagined Billy Graham receiving an introduction like that. I climbed the three steps up to the platform and walked across to the lectern in the centre. I began by giving some customary words of thanks to the pastor for his 'very kind welcome', introduced myself to the people and then proceeded to preach my shiny new sermon with its three major points, each containing six sub-points. After preaching for around twenty-five minutes, I drew to a close and gave an appeal for those who wanted to become Christians. Four people responded – which I was absolutely delighted with. I prayed a simple prayer for the four respondents, after which I picked up my sermon notes, vacated the platform and happily walked back to my seat on the front row, somewhat relieved that my job was now done. Little did I know that my night was only about to begin.

The elderly pastor left his seat and made his way over to where I was sitting. With as much discretion as a polar bear suffering from a headache, he whispered loudly, 'Why are you sitting down?'

'What do you mean?' I replied.

'You haven't finished yet,' he said.

'I have finished,' I responded.

'No, you haven't,' he said with a stern voice. 'You've yet to pray for people to receive miracles.'

Using all the diplomacy I could muster, I attempted to reason with the old man of God, but to no avail. I whispered, 'Well, I don't really do that kind of thing, you see . . .' But before I could utter another word, he interrupted me. 'Well you'd better do it tonight,' he said. 'We've advertised that you will pray for people to receive miracles. Do you really think these people came just to hear you preach? Get onto that platform and get on with it!'

The Return Journey

I broke into a cold sweat as I realized I was left with little choice but to return to the platform. Shaking from head to foot, I stood up and began to walk towards the stage. Although it was only a few metres away, it felt like the longest walk I'd ever taken in my life. Twenty-one years of living flashed before my eyes as I made my way with fear and trepidation. The walk to the platform twenty-five minutes earlier had been relatively easy, albeit a little nerve-racking. At least then I had a good idea of what was going to happen next. But this time it was completely different. I was now entering uncharted territory for which I was totally unprepared, as I was required to pray for people to receive miracles. I felt totally out of my comfort zone and had no idea how this would pan out.

I climbed back onto the platform, walked to the lectern and nervously looked out over the congregation. For a few agonizing moments, my mind went totally blank: I had no idea what to say next. The spectacle of a young preacher lost for words left the audience in bemused silence. But after what seemed a lifetime, I somehow managed to gather my thoughts and remembered what the elderly minister had told me to do. Speaking gently and quietly into the microphone, I timidly announced, 'Ah, by the way, if anyone would like prayer, please come forward now.'

At first, it looked as though I might have got away with it, as no one seemed to respond. But my relief was short-lived, as slowly but surely sounds of footsteps began coming my way. There were only a few to begin with, but that soon changed as literally half the congregation made their way to the front. At this point, I felt like I needed prayer for healing myself, as I was convinced I was about to have a panic attack.

I stood silently and watched a sea of faces all coming in my direction. I distinctly remember feeling completely daunted by the idea that these people were actually expecting the power of God to be manifested through little me. Convinced they would be disappointed, I quickly formed an exit strategy in my mind, glancing to see where the nearest fire exit was so I could make a quick getaway in the likely event of an emergency.

Take the Walking Frame Away

As the crowd stood at the front, a middle-aged woman among them caught my eye. She was leaning on a walking frame and was bent over in great pain. I later learned that she had major spinal problems which would eventually confine her to a wheelchair. I don't know why, but I decided to pray for her first. I came off the stage, made my way over to her and laid my hands on her head. The first words of my prayer were, 'Lord, it would be wonderful if this lady could be healed.' The next line included a little King James English, which always tends to make prayers sound more spiritual: 'Lord, if it be thy will, thou canst heal thy daughter.' Nice words – but there really wasn't a lot of faith going on. It was as if my jargon-filled prayer was suggesting a technical 'miracle clause' somewhere in the Bible, but it just wasn't going to happen under my ministry tonight. However, what happened in the next few minutes was something I genuinely didn't expect.

Suddenly, in the middle of my gentle prayer, God spoke to me. It wasn't an audible voice but an unmistakable still, small voice that was as clear as clear can be. I know that's a strong statement, but there is no other way of describing it. The voice said to me, 'Take this woman's walking frame away.' It was so distinct and profound that I felt compelled to obey. You may wonder why I'm so sure this was God speaking. The answer is simple: I really wouldn't have told myself to do that.

So I acted on what I heard God tell me to do. I removed the walking frame on which the woman was leaning and set it to one side. Deprived of her support, she lost her balance and nearly fell over. I grabbed hold of her in the nick of time and held on to her. I would love to tell you she was instantly healed. But that's not what happened. That would be too easy – and besides, God likes to make life interesting for us, don't you think?

After I removed the walking frame, nothing happened for well over one minute. Of course, when you're standing in front of a crowd who are focusing intensely on you, one minute is a very long time. During this period, the woman held firmly on to me – and if I'm honest, I gripped her tightly too. I remember watching her curious eyes staring at me inquisitively, as if to say, 'What are you going to do next?' I then looked out at the congregation, who also gazed at me with pondering eyes, asking, 'What is he going to do next?'

Meanwhile, the elderly pastor who was leading the event stood behind me on the platform. I thought it might be a good idea to give him a quick glance, thinking he would give me a look of encouragement and approval. But I was not encouraged when I turned round and saw him staring intensely back at me with one eye open and one eye shut. It was clear what he was thinking: 'If this works, you will be back. If this doesn't work, you'll need a walking frame yourself by the time I've finished with you.'

Healed

After one minute of absolute nothingness, something shocking and mind-boggling happened right before my eyes. The woman who I was praying for suddenly jolted. Then her bent-over body began to slowly straighten up until she was completely upright. Quietly, she turned round, faced away from me and began to walk. It was a slow pace at first but she got faster and faster until she began to run all round the auditorium. Members of the congregation began to clap their hands and cheer at the sight of the woman, now jumping and leaping for joy. She had been healed – just like that!

I was in a kind of daze. The roller coaster of emotions I'd just experienced had worn me out and I was worried I might be hallucinating. But I wasn't. With my own eyes I had witnessed something that was nothing short of a miracle. One minute, she was bent over in agony and dependent on a walking frame – the next, she was pain-free and no longer needing any support. It truly was astonishing.

At the end of the service the pastor came to me with his diary already open, wanting to arrange my next visit. After we had agreed the date, he smiled and said, 'I look forward to seeing you next time, then' – words I had thought I'd never hear again.

Conviction

And so began my journey into the miraculous. From that night, God created a conviction in my heart to believe for miracles to accompany my communication of his good news. I decided that from that point on I would pray for people at every church where I was invited to speak. And that's exactly what I did. Perhaps I was a little naïve at times, especially as some churches were not used to having visiting speakers lay hands on members of the congregation. But no one ever objected. More to the point, the results spoke for themselves. Story after story emerged of people receiving miracles. Word began to spread and invitations came in from all over the UK asking me to speak at evangelistic events where people could receive prayer. I accepted all of them. It really didn't matter to me whether they were large or small churches. I was just delighted to have the opportunity of communicating the good news of Jesus Christ and praying for people to experience his miraculous power.

Stories of miracles became front-page news in some of the towns and cities I visited. I even made a number of appearances on local television and radio stations at which I gave interviews that were received very favourably. I was honoured to address some Christian conferences, speaking on the theme of signs and wonders. Doors also began to open for me to preach at huge meetings in different parts of the world, including Africa and Asia. Most importantly of all, more and more unchurched people attended the events where I was invited to speak, sometimes forming up to 70 per cent of the audience. Some came out of curiosity, others because of scepticism, and still more because of personal circumstances. But they came, and many of them left having experienced the greatest miracle of all: in the words of the well-known hymn, ransomed, healed, restored, forgiven.

Steps

There are three important steps that those who desire to experience the miraculous need to take in order to move in the right direction:

The first step takes you out of your comfort zone

This is a huge challenge for many of us. It means being willing to move away from the safety and security of the familiar and trusting someone else to lead you instead, going where you haven't been before. For me, the first step into the miraculous was totally unexpected, something I didn't feel prepared for. Yet while my experience is undoubtedly unique, the principle is the same for everyone. It is a requirement to have complete and utter faith in God, no matter what circumstances seem to be before you. But like the mother eagle who swoops down to catch her eaglets when they're learning to fly, the Lord is always there for you. He is your guide and it's a matter of believing in him, confident that he knows the way ahead.

The second step takes you into the unknown

Seeing more of the miraculous is a journey. Each miracle is different, just as every leaf has a distinct design and all fingerprints are uniquely lined. This is where courage must rise up. Some miracles are spectacular. Others aren't. Some involve deliverance *from* circumstances while others are to do with provision of strength to go *through* challenges.

The third step takes you beyond yourself

A miracle is an extraordinary event initiated by divine authority. It doesn't happen by the abilities of humans but comes about by the power of God. Yet there are undoubted instances of human faith playing an important role in seeing the miraculous happen, even if reason is challenged in the process. We do well to heed the wise words of Proverbs 3:5, 'Trust in the LORD with all your heart and lean not on your own understanding.'

Relevant

The late George Harrison, a member of The Beatles, was a spiritual seeker all his life. He once stated, 'The purpose of life is to find out "Who am I?", "Why am I here?" and "Where am I going?"' What he was saying is that most people's life quest is to discover identity, purpose and destiny. He was right: it's just that so many people seek all the *right* things in all the *wrong* places. Yet in Christianity lies the answer: Jesus Christ. Not a religion but a person. He offers reality, fulfilment and wholeness. In him we find identity, purpose and destiny. People flocked to Jesus because they saw someone who was authentic, who offered genuine solutions to their real needs. Christ's message has not changed. He is the same yesterday, today and for ever.

While western culture is generally not enamoured of dry Christianity, I've found that the vast majority of unchurched people I've spoken to are open to God. They're searching for wholeness, longing for fulfilment and desperate for reality, but they just don't know where to find it. C.S. Lewis astutely observed that many people are blind to the obvious and so need something to get their attention.

In an age that is closed to organized religion but open to the spiritual, the church needs to rediscover its God-given mandate to minister in the miraculous. To do so is to demonstrate signs to make people wonder – so that they may be shaken from their doubts and disbelief and come in awe and wonder to the God of wonder, who longs to know them and restore them into an eternal friendship with himself.

Do you want to see more miracles? If you do, you must live with a conviction that nothing is too difficult with God, no matter how daunting the situation. He's looking for people of faith. Clever arguments and endless debates are not going to make a difference in a world that's in desperate need. But people who know what it is to see the power of God manifested through their lives will. When Jesus died on the cross and rose again from the dead, he made it possible for us to receive his forgiveness, and his ascension made way for the Holy Spirit to come, so that every Christian can be empowered to carry on his work. Miracles are an intrinsic part of God's good news. The possibilities of what God can do through a person who is truly full of his Spirit are endless. Let the journey begin.

2

GOD OF MIRACLES

In a day of huge technological advances, life, on the surface at least, has never been so good. The dawning of the communication age has revolutionized how the world works, making it a smaller and more accessible place in which to live. Medical science has seen many breakthroughs in the fight against disease and sickness. People are more health-conscious than they've ever been and are living longer than ever before, with life expectancy predicted to rise substantially by 2050.

Yet despite all our twenty-first-century achievements, people are aware that there is only so much that human technology can do. Sickness still exists. Stress-related conditions are on the up. Concerns about climate change and what the future holds are foremost in many people's hearts. Many are preoccupied with financial worries, conscious that all it would take is one catastrophic incident for their money to be lost for good. And, of course, there's the constant lurking menace of terrorism, creating a sense of genuine fear and apprehension around the world.

Openness

So have people today lost sight of spirituality? Do they no longer believe in miracles, feeling equipped by modern technology to deal with any problem that comes their way? I doubt it. Far from rejecting a belief in miracles, more people than ever are convinced that they can still happen. African and Asian cultures are already largely given to strong belief in the realm of the supernatural. However, this is now increasingly the case with many people in the western world too. For example, 79 per cent of people polled by Harris in America during November 2007 said they believed in miracles. Even in so-called secular Britain, one in five adults believes that 'prayer changes the world' (Tearfund survey, November 2007).

What's going on, then? In all probability there is a greater openness to Christianity than ever before. Of course this is not always outwardly obvious. In Britain, for example, many churches have become discouraged by the lack of attendance, with only around 7 per cent of people regularly bothering to turn up. But it would be a mistake to interpret this as a rejection of God. Statistics consistently show that while fewer go to church, as many as 70 per cent of British people believe in God. Maybe they have rejected organized Christianity as they've had it presented to them, but there is openness among them. So often, the church has failed to invest in that openness by not engaging meaningfully with them.

Miracles in the Bible

Miracles are a very important aspect of scripture. Throughout the Old Testament there are numerous accounts of them happening, too many to include in this book. For example, Moses led the children of Israel to deliverance via a dry path that God created through the sea. In another incident, Elijah was miraculously taken up into heaven in a whirlwind. And what about Naaman, who was commanded by Elijah's successor Elisha to dip in the river Jordan seven times and was subsequently healed of leprosy? Or the astonishing story of Daniel, who was thrown into a den of vicious lions but emerged without so much as a mark on his body because God had shut their mouths? These are just a tiny sample of the extraordinary events that happened in the Old Testament.

Miracles were an intrinsic part of Jesus' ministry too. He healed incurable diseases, raised dead people back to life, turned water into fine wine, fed more than five thousand people using five loaves and two fish, released those oppressed by demonic possession – and the list goes on. If the amount of space an author takes to write about a particular subject is an indication of its importance, then the writers of the gospels must have viewed miracles as highly significant. Matthew devotes 44 per cent of his gospel to Jesus' miracles, Mark 29 per cent, Luke 30 per cent and John 30 per cent.

Why Jesus was Such a Draw

Let's turn back the clock two thousand years and look at the world in which Jesus lived. It was a very different situation to the one we see today. There were no cars and no easy forms of alternative communication. International travel was generally by boat and took weeks, if not months, to complete. There were no games consoles, and television didn't figure in anybody's imagination. It really was a much more primitive place.

Yet, despite the huge variations between then and now, people in Jesus' time had a surprising amount in common with us today. Their basic needs were very much the same. They could get sick. They had financial worries. They had concerns about what the future might hold. People in those days lived very busy lives, just as we do today. Some succeeded and became rich. Others struggled to get by, living a poor and meagre existence. Some were powerful and some were weak. There was crime, violence, fear, social problems, and much more besides.

So what was it about Jesus that drew the crowds to him? Why might someone take time out of their busy schedule in order to go and listen to him? What would be the point of going through all that hassle just to see one man? Here are two reasons why Jesus was so compelling:

First, what he said made a lot of sense. People compared Jesus' message with that of the religious establishment, and while the Pharisees seemed interested only in intellectual stimulation, Jesus communicated profound truth in a way that they could understand and engage with. The Pharisees once accused him of being a 'friend of sinners'. They meant this as an insult, but they were unwittingly paying him the ultimate compliment – recognizing that he could connect with ordinary people and they couldn't. The only way they knew how to influence people was through fear and manipulation.

Second, Jesus was compelling because he met people's needs. Multitudes of people will show up when they know a genuine miracle-worker is in town. And Jesus was no disappointment. He healed the sick and did the impossible. Not once did Jesus ever need to advertise himself – the miracles did all that for him. Nor did he preach lots of sermons on the miraculous – he just got on with helping others experience them.

In addition to all the miracles recorded in the gospels, John finishes his account of Jesus' life with a very interesting thought. He says, 'Jesus did many other things as well. If every one of them were written down, I suppose that even the whole world would not have room for the books that would be written' (John 21:25).

Different Times – Same Message

Before his ascension, Jesus actually commissioned his disciples to 'go into all the world and preach the good news'. He also told them to expect miraculous 'signs' to accompany their proclamation of the message (Mark 16:15–18). Of course, some theologians view this latter aspect of the Mark 16 Great Commission as only applicable to the disciples Jesus was speaking to at that particular time. They suggest that miracles of the kind that happened in the New Testament were only to be manifested in the apostolic era, which ceased with the passing of the twelve apostles. However, those who hold to charismatic theology argue against cessationism, believing that the apostolic age continues until Christ's return (though eschatological viewpoints differ hugely) and that miracles can and should be expected today. Charismatic churches are certainly among the fastest growing in the world. While some may dismiss modern-day claims of miracles as mere coincidences, we do well to remember the words of former Archbishop of Canterbury William Temple, who said, 'When we pray, coincidences happen.'

I have always disapproved of those who disparage theological study, having spent three years at a seminary myself. Paul the apostle even encouraged his young protégé Timothy to 'study to show yourself approved'. However, simply knowing the theory of the Bible isn't good enough, as this alone provides no answers for a world that's in great need. It really must be accompanied by practise and experience. People today are looking for answers, and I'm convinced the Bible provides hope. That's not to say that there are easy solutions for every problem which people encounter. There aren't. However, it is not unreasonable to believe that God still works miraculously today.

Miracles can sometimes be spectacular, but this is not always the case. Some are big, while others seem small: some major, others apparently minor. At times they can involve deliverance *from* struggles and difficulties, but they can also provide people with supernatural courage to go *through* their challenges, no matter how impossible the circumstances might seem.

Sometimes they happen expectedly, sometimes not, but whichever way they come about, no two are ever the same. They're as vast in variety as the stars in the sky. Yet when they do occur, there is always an ultimate purpose for each one. Every true miracle unfailingly points to the Lordship of Jesus Christ, the Son of the living God. In truth, miracles are signs that are designed to cause people to wonder, drawing them to see a higher authority that is in ultimate control.

This book is not a quick-fix guide to guaranteed results. Life just isn't that simple. However, I want to encourage you to see that God's power has not changed. The same God who did miracles in the Bible still does miracles in the twenty-first century.

On my travels to hundreds of venues as an evangelist, I've found that unchurched people I talk to are hungry for miracles, and their appetite is growing. For example,

I am amazed at the number of medical doctors who come to events where I communicate the Gospel and publicly pray for people to be healed. I asked one doctor why she thought so many physicians attended events like this. 'It's simple,' she said. 'We are more aware than anybody of the limitations of the medical profession.'

Why Miracles Can Still Happen

Before moving on to how we might experience more of the miraculous in our lives, let's establish why it is reasonable for Christians to believe that miracles can still happen today. Here are five reasons:

1. Miracles express who God is

I once heard someone provocatively say, 'God does not "do" miracles.' I immediately questioned the statement in my mind, but listened to the reasoning behind it and strangely found myself in agreement. We consider what God does as 'miraculous' because we view it from a perspective of human limitation, seeing it as out of the ordinary. However, miracles are not abnormal for God. What we consider 'miracles' are totally normal for him, in fact he's not even trying when they happen. He only does what he does because he is who he is. His *doing* comes out of his *being*. He is the source of all living things. Everything about him communicates life. So when he speaks, his word is compelled to come to pass. As soon as God declares it, it's as good as done. Romans 4:17 says God 'calls things that are not as though they were'. It's as easy for God to speak life into being as it is for you to pick up this book and read it. We consider it miraculous – God considers it normal. In the creation story in

Genesis 1, God's simple command was 'Let it be' and it came to pass. It's because he is God that nothing is impossible.

There are three terms used by theologians to describe God: omnipotent, omniscient and omnipresent.

God is omnipotent (all-powerful) – he has ultimate power and authority. It's not that he has been given these things, but they are reflections of who he is. Psalm 90:2 says he is 'from everlasting to everlasting'. Therefore, nothing is impossible with him. He holds the key to every problem and challenge that comes our way.

God is omniscient (all-knowing). He doesn't acquire knowledge by learning, because he knows everything. There is nothing that he isn't aware of. He doesn't just have answers to human problems – he is the answer. So that's why he can meet every need, no matter how complex it seems.

God is omnipresent (all-present) – he's not restricted by time and space. He is everywhere at every time. This is a mystery that we find difficult to comprehend with our minds, but he is without limitation. Distance really isn't an issue for God.

2. *Miracles are signs of God's immanence and transcendence*

Many miracles are to do with God's immanence – his involvement in natural processes. These are natural miracles which can be seen in creation, for example the miracle of life, the miracle of a newborn baby, the miracle of gravity, the miracle of plants, flowers, trees etc. However, there are also miracles that relate to God's transcendence – his involvement outside nature. In essence, these are supernatural miracles, extraordinary occurrences – defying nature and not limited by its processes. There really are no limits with God.

3. Miracles are the foundation of Christianity

It's impossible to be a Christian without a belief in the miraculous. This may sound a strong statement but it is not unreasonable. After all, Christians are people who believe that Jesus died on the cross and rose again on the third day. The very foundation of our faith is a belief that he really was resurrected.

It's worth noting the difference between being raised from death and resurrection. For example, Lazarus was raised from the dead. But utterly breathtaking as this miracle was, it was for a limited period of time, perhaps another thirty years, and then he would die again. Jesus, however, was resurrected. This wasn't just a temporary measure. He lives for evermore. In fact, even now he reigns in the power of his resurrection, and that's the very reason why Christians around the world worship him. There would be no point in worshipping someone who's dead. But Jesus is alive.

Paul speaks frankly about this in 1 Corinthians 15:17, saying, 'If Christ has not been raised, your faith is futile; you are still in your sins.' From here, he goes on to write about the resurrection that Christians will experience after they die, through which mortality will be replaced with immortality and death will be defeated once and for all. That's why every Christian has a miraculous hope that goes beyond the grave. No wonder Paul says, 'Thanks be to God! He gives us the victory through our Lord Jesus Christ' (1 Cor. 15:57).

The truth of death and resurrection is a profound mystery: that God through Christ (who is immortal) should be born as a man, die on a cross and rise again from the grave in order to bring about the reconciliation of humans with God. Thus Jesus made possible the greatest miracle of all – the gift of salvation. Romans 1:16 says the Gospel 'is the power of God for the salvation of everyone who believes'.

Christians, therefore, are those who believe in the miraculous and have first-hand experience too.

4. Miracles are still experienced by millions of people

This is an important proof that miracles still happen today. Countless thousands of people believe they have received them – and surely they can't all be wrong? A good example of this for me is the story of Sandra Hesp. In 2003, she was invited by a friend to attend an event where I was speaking in Derbyshire. She was totally unchurched and very sceptical about Christianity, doubting the very existence of God. However, after speaking, I offered to pray for people to experience healing. Sandra had suffered from a painful back condition for a number of years, and she was in great pain during the event. Her friend managed to convince her to come forward for prayer. She thought, 'What have I got to lose?' So she went to the front, and after being prayed for she was amazed to find that the pain had completely gone. This was the beginning of a journey that eventually led Sandra to personal faith in Christ. She has never been the same since, totally pain-free and a Christian who is fully committed to her local church. Sandra insists that had it not been for her initially experiencing the miracle of healing, she would never have thought of coming to personal faith in Jesus Christ and receiving the ultimate miracle, forgiveness.

You simply can't deny people's experiences like that. Or take the case of Carol from Leicester, who wrote to me, giving me permission to use her story as a testimony to God's healing. Carol had a condition known as angiosarcoma – an aggressive blood cancer which spreads very quickly throughout the body. She was given very little hope by her doctors, who knew only too well the seriousness of her situation. However, she came to an event where I was speaking and afterwards received prayer. As I prayed for her, I felt God prompt me to tell her, 'When the doctors notice a small improvement, you will experience complete healing so that you will not require an operation.' Within the space of a few weeks, Carol got word from her doctor that there had been a minor improvement. From then on, she kept trusting in what she'd felt God had said, eventually receiving word that the condition had completely cleared up and that there would be no need for her to have surgery.

Just two examples from among many thousands of people who have no doubt that they have experienced nothing less than a miracle.

5. Miracles still happen because God has not changed

The world is constantly changing. Each generation experiences the benefits of technological advances as well as the new challenges they bring. But one thing's for sure – whatever happens in this world, God does not change. He doesn't need to. His word is still the same. His power is not diminished. His authority is unchallenged. He's still the same God who brought miraculous deliverance to the children of Israel time and time again. He's exactly the same one who healed sick and oppressed people as he walked the earth two thousand years ago. And because his power is undiminished today, he is still able to heal the sick, deliver the oppressed, free the captives, restore sight, unstop deafness and even raise the dead. Why not?

Time to See God

If we are going to experience more of the miraculous in our lives, we need to have a vision of who God is. Isaiah caught a glimpse of his glory in Isaiah 6, and that one encounter changed his entire life. Often, there needs to be a revelation of God which challenges us to see that he is greater than we ever thought and more powerful than we imagined. In Paul's letter to the Ephesians he prays that the believers 'may be filled to the measure of all the fullness of God'. He explains that this is the same God who is able to 'do immeasurably more than all we ask or imagine, according to his power that is at work within us' (Eph. 3:19–20).

On a trip to India some years ago, I took an internal flight to a small airport, where I was picked up by some pastors. From there, they drove me to the venue where I was to speak. Since I'd already travelled a long way that day, I thought it would be helpful to know how far we had yet to go, because the last thing I wanted was a long drive on bumpy Indian roads. I asked the driver, 'How long will it take to get to our destination?' He replied, 'Oh, no problem, just a short journey. No problem.' This cheered me up. I estimated in my mind that it would take no more than twenty minutes. So we drove, and twenty minutes passed. Then thirty minutes passed, and forty, and fifty. Then it turned into one hour, then two, then three, then six, then eight. After nine hours, I asked the driver, 'Are we nearly there yet?' That was without doubt the longest 'short journey' I had ever taken in my life!

We drove up a lonely mountain road until long after sunset and eventually reached a point where the road was impassable by jeep. So we had to get out of the vehicle and walk through a forest area in order to get to the village where I was to be the preacher.

We finally reached the venue. It was almost at the top of a mountain. But just before entering the building, I happened to glance up to the heavens, and as I did, I was taken aback by what I saw. It was the most incredible sight I have ever seen. A starry sky, vast and awesome – yet so close, it was as if I could have reached out my hand and touched the stars. It was truly awe-inspiring. Suddenly Psalm 19:1 came into my thoughts: 'The heavens declare the glory of God.' As I stood there, I could visualise as never before the sheer greatness of who God is. A voice spoke into my spirit, saying, 'This is your God. This is your God.' Creation tells us something about who God is, his power, his magnificence, his might. That sight inspired me beyond what words could describe.

As I gazed upwards, my interpreter said to me, 'Come, we must go into the meeting. They are waiting for you.' I asked him, 'Who exactly am I speaking to tonight?' He replied, 'Fifty per cent of the people are Hindu and fifty per cent are Muslim. They have come because they want to know what a white man looks like.' Far from being daunted, I relished the opportunity. I knew that God was with me, the same one who spoke the stars into the sky by the authority of his word.

I entered the small building to find it jam-packed with people. As I stood up to speak, I had no feelings of fear or intimidation, just an assured confidence in the greatness of the God who I spoke about. I was addressing the people as God's ambassador and I knew he was with me. That night, I told the people about the incredible splendour of Jesus, who died on a cross and rose again from the dead. As I spoke, there was a tangible sense of his presence that I had never before experienced. That night, hundreds of people gave their lives to Jesus and there were outstanding miracles as I prayed for people. I will never forget it as long as I live. What happened? I just saw God being himself: God.

He's the source of miracles. His miraculous manifestations are not performances designed to impress but a reflection of who he is. It is for this reason more than any other that we should expect signs and wonders to happen today. God is longing to reveal more and more of himself to us. It's when we have a deeper revelation of his greatness that we'll understand more of his power. It's not about seeing the bigness of the circumstance, but about having a vision of the Lord who is so much bigger than any problem or difficulty we can face in life. And he is for us, not against us. That's why there is every reason for us to believe for miracles today. Our God really is the God of miracles.

3

FOUNDATIONS FOR THE MIRACULOUS

Have you ever been at sea during a storm? I have, and I can vouch for the fact that it really isn't a lot of fun.

A few days before Christmas 2002, I was travelling to Ireland to spend the holidays with my family. Since I had lots of presents to bring with me, I decided it would make much more sense to sail across instead of flying. The most convenient place to catch a car ferry was the port of Stranraer in Scotland. From there, it's only around a two-hour trip to Belfast harbour. When I arrived in Stranraer, the weather was very unsettled. There were gusty winds and it even began to snow. I actually didn't expect to set sail on that cold winter's night, as conditions were deteriorating. But to my surprise, I was told to board the ferry and that everything was on time.

The ship left port and began the crossing. I took my seat on the upper deck, relieved that we had got going. Since I hadn't seen my family in a while, I was really looking forward to being with them again soon. But little did I know what lay ahead that evening.

Not long into the crossing, the storm took a turn for the worse, reaching gale force. It was utterly ferocious.

I've never experienced anything like it. Waves lashed right up to the windows, chairs were dislodged from their set positions and cups smashed on the floor as the ferry was shaken around. Passengers tried as hard as they could to hold on to their own seats, as if in a rodeo competition. That ship was tossed about the Irish Sea as if the raging ocean held it in complete contempt. Everyone on board was terrified. There was screaming, shouting, crying, vomiting – and that was just me!

What should have been a two-hour journey took well over ten hours to complete. The storm didn't let up for a long time. When the ferry eventually did arrive in Belfast, I drove off it with a huge sigh of relief, thankful to God that I was still alive, though mentally still bobbing up and down as if I were on a water bed. It had been a truly frightening journey, one I hope I'll never have to repeat.

A Strange Sight on a Stormy Night

I can imagine, therefore, how scary it must have been for the disciples when they faced storms at sea. Matthew 14 records one such occasion, when their boat was a considerable distance from land. The wind blew strongly against them and the waves buffeted their vessel vigorously, making it virtually impossible for them to make any progress. It was a dangerous situation. Yet, in the midst of it all, their attention was strangely shifted away from the storm to something even more frightening in the distance. As they gazed out, they glimpsed a sight that human eyes had never before seen. Someone (or something) was walking on the water. Concerned as they were by the storm, this paled into insignificance in comparison to the sheer terror they felt at this dreadful sight. They thought it was a ghost, and cried out in fear (Matt. 14:26). Imagine that – a bunch of tough men, some of whom were known as 'sons of thunder', crying like babies because they thought they'd seen a ghost!

Suddenly the distant figure on the water spoke, saying, 'Take courage. It is I. Don't be afraid.' It was a familiar sound – the voice of the one they'd given up everything to follow. Yes, it was Jesus, taking an early morning stroll on the water. Yet most of the disciples remained unconvinced it could really be him. At this point, Peter, the fumbling spokesman for the group of sailors, spoke out. He had a habit of saying the wrong thing at the worst possible moment. On this occasion, it's not difficult to imagine the rest of the disciples trying to place their hands over his mouth to silence him as he sought to communicate with the strange being in the distance. But to no avail. Peter said, 'Lord, if it's you, tell me to come to you on the water.' Jesus replied with one word: 'Come.'

Depending on your viewpoint, Peter's response was either very brave or incredibly brash. But the fact is that he stepped out over the side of the boat and began to walk towards Jesus. It's hard to imagine what must have gone through the minds of the rest of the disciples at this point. Perhaps confusion, amazement, bewilderment, bemusement – who knows? But the fact is that Peter made history by becoming only the second person ever to walk on water – a miracle.

It's interesting that this miracle happened during a storm. Living in the realm of the miraculous is not a guarantee of a life without trials. But this one incident provides us with an invaluable insight, highlighting some vital foundations which we can learn from in our own pursuit of the miraculous.

1. The Word

Did Peter merely walk on water? Of course, physically he did. But there is a deeper foundation to the miracle. Peter actually walked on Jesus' word. After all, Jesus' command was that Peter should 'come'. Remember, this is the same Jesus who spoke the word and caused the stars to appear in the sky. So a simple 'Come' from Jesus was enough for Peter to defy the laws of physics and tread the waves. Surely one word from Jesus is enough to carry us through every circumstance and challenge of life, no matter how tempestuous it may be.

The word of God is the most important and significant component of a divine miracle. God's miracles are always intrinsically based on what he says. They're not rooted in human presumption or speculation. Herein lies a vital key: knowing what God has said is a clear sign that our miracle is as good as accomplished. From this point on, it's a matter of walking on the word. So many people never experience the miraculous because they haven't listened to the voice of God, and therefore their faith is not based on a proper foundation. Disappointment is inevitable when the basis of what someone believes for is other than God's word. I've spoken to many people who feel disillusioned because the thing they believed would happen didn't come to pass as they'd hoped. I always ask, 'What was the basis on which you believed it?' – and often it's had nothing to do with anything God has said. The simple way to avoid disillusionment is to make sure you don't get illusioned! Walk on the word.

But how do we receive the word of God? Does it come by personal prophecy or through other gifts of the Holy Spirit? Of course, God can speak to us through these things. However, the primary way we receive it is through taking time to read the Bible. This daily discipline will help us develop sensitivity to what God is saying to us. Nevertheless, hearing his word is not enough in itself. We've got to listen carefully to what God is saying to us through it. An old music teacher of mine used to teach me the difference between hearing and listening. 'Hearing is passive – listening is active,' he said.

When we read the Bible, it is vitally important that we actively listen to what God is saying and then use that as the foundation. After all, God's word is the carrier. While in one sense it is true that Peter walked on the water, it is even truer that Jesus' word is what carried Peter on the water. That's the real miracle.

2. Trust

Faith is a natural progression from receiving the word of God. Romans 10:17 says, 'The point is, before you trust, you have to listen' (*The Message*). It's about listening to what God says and then taking him at his word. So that's exactly what Peter did. Climbing out of the boat was a totally illogical action as far as human reason was concerned. After all, how silly is it to do such a ridiculous thing during calm weather, never mind a raging storm? Nevertheless, Peter acted on Christ's command. When Jesus said, 'Come,' he probably wasn't directing his word only to Peter, but to all the disciples in the boat. Each of them had the same chance to walk on the water and experience a miracle for themselves. Yet only Peter took the opportunity. It's easy to look back and celebrate his historic moment, but the chances are that if you had been one of the disciples, you would probably have stayed inside the boat along with all the rest. So many Christians receive a word from God but never climb out of the comfort zone and actually walk on it. James said, 'Faith without action is dead.'

Unbelief is the most important barrier preventing us from experiencing the miraculous. A whole generation of Israelites missed out on the 'promised land' because of their refusal to have faith. It's one thing to believe something in your head, but quite another to progressively pursue the purpose of God by faith. God isn't looking for more theorists. There are plenty of those around. It's practitioners he's looking for. That is to say people who count the cost and still dare to venture towards the promised land. Surely that's what living by faith is all about.

Remember, when God says something, he always makes it happen. So trust his word. Miracles simply don't happen unless we walk by faith on that foundation.

3. Obedience

Obedience is also a natural progression from faith and the word of God. 1 Samuel 15:22 says, 'To obey is better than sacrifice.' In other words, God is more interested in us serving him as sons and daughters than in us sacrificing for him as slaves. Obedience denotes the idea of willingness rather than obligation.

So when Jesus said, 'Come,' Peter could have responded by saying something like, 'Jesus, just give me a few moments so I can think about this.' He then might have thought through the consequences of stepping out of the boat and doing as Jesus had commanded. For example, his reputation would tell him, 'What if you climb out of the boat and it all goes wrong?' His ego would say, 'What will the other disciples think if you do this?' His fear would remind him, 'Don't do it. It's never happened before – so it won't work for you.' His mind would advise him, 'Walking on water is a physical impossibility, so don't even think about leaving the boat.'

But Peter's response was nothing like that. For all his imperfections, there's something endearing about Simon Peter. It's as if he climbed out of the boat enthusiastically, with an excitable childlike faith, knowing that Jesus loved him and would be there for him all the way. Characters like Peter are much needed in the twenty-first-century church. Of course, they make mistakes and get it wrong at times. But God can use people like that. Better to throw caution to the wind and launch out by faith than to bob up and down in the same harbour for years. Better to have one Peter with an enthusiastic faith who dares to believe for the miraculous than a church full of 'play it safe' Christians who relish comfort and never experience the reality of who God really is.

God is desperate for you to experience his miraculous power. Therefore, when you listen to his word being spoken into your life, remember that anything he says is ultimately for your benefit. Sometimes his word requires us to repent, which means to change direction. Sometimes he challenges us to deal with certain issues so that blockages that prevent us from receiving a miracle can be removed from our lives. Whatever he tells you to do – obey him willingly, knowing he will not withhold any good thing from you.

4. Courage

As the disciples cried out in fear at the sight of what they thought was a ghost in the distance, Jesus tried to reassure them by saying, 'Take courage' and 'Don't be afraid.' However, the only person who seemed to receive this was Peter, since he was the only one who got out of the boat and walked towards Jesus. The rest looked on. They saw the miracle of walking on water but never experienced it for themselves. Too many Christians observe history being made instead of being courageous enough to make it themselves.

Millions of people today don't experience God's miraculous power, because they lack the courage to step out and believe God will do what he has said he will do. They prefer to be spectators rather than participators. Why is that? Fear is often the issue. Fear is caused by past negative experiences. For example, people who have been involved in a road traffic accident are often afraid to drive again. But the best way to overcome fear is to get back behind the wheel of a car and start driving as soon as possible. The longer you leave it, the harder it becomes.

'Been there, done that, bought the T-shirt' is the cynical sentiment expressed by people embedded in lives that lack courage. The problem is often that the T-shirt they wear is old and worn. At the very least, they ought to try something new so they can get a new T-shirt.

The harbour is a relatively easy place to live. But miracles don't usually happen there. It's at sea that they occur. It is safe and sheltered in the bay. You don't really need a miracle behind the protection of the harbour wall. But the ocean can be torrid and tempestuous. Miracles happen in the lives of men and women who live by the courage of their convictions and dare to journey through the rough waters of life towards their God-given destiny. Anyone who has ever done anything of significance in life has at some point been required to act courageously. For example, Alexander Bell kept on trying to invent the telephone despite criticism that it would never work. Today we take it for granted – but he didn't. Rosa Parks dared to believe for civil rights in America at a time when African-Americans were treated as second-class citizens. John Wesley demonstrated remarkable courage when he rode through Britain on horseback and preached the Gospel against a background of terrible opposition.

If you want to experience the miraculous in your life, you have to be courageous enough to walk on God's word – even during storms.

5. Revelation

When the disciples were overcome with fear on seeing a 'ghost' on the water, Jesus had to remind them, 'It is I.' In other words, he was saying, 'What are you worrying about? It's only me! Who else could possibly do this?' Yet apart from Peter, the disciples still didn't really believe it was Jesus. Surely if they had, they would have left the boat along with Peter and experienced the miracle of walking on water for themselves. But they didn't realize it was him.

Deeper revelation is a key component to seeing the miraculous. But the type of revelation we need is not a glimpse of what the future holds. God rarely reveals the path that lies ahead. If he did, it would be too much for us: we would want to quit with immediate effect because the challenges before us would be so daunting. Revelation that leads to miraculous breakthroughs relates to who God is – his character and his glory. God only does what he does because he is who he is. He said, 'I am the Lord who heals you,' because this is a revelation of who he is – the healer. Nothing is impossible with him. It's when we have a vision of God for who he really is that we begin to see him work through us. The effect of revelation on us is a greater confidence in God's power and authority over every situation.

On a tour of Africa a few years ago, I was invited to speak at a meeting of many thousands of people. A big percentage of the people in that meeting were non-believers. The reason why they were coming was that adverts had gone up all round their town declaring, 'Evangelist Roy Todd will pray for you to receive a miracle!' As we travelled to the venue, I felt daunted and weak. It was as if I were carrying the entire pressure of the event on myself. Then I heard God say to me, 'The pressure isn't yours to bear. You are not a performer but a carrier of my presence.' Suddenly I realized the force of what God was saying. I prayed, 'Lord, give me a greater revelation of who you are – and permit me to carry a greater sense of your presence than I've ever had before into that meeting tonight.'

I preached at the meeting and the glory of God was utterly tangible. At the end, many found faith in Christ and astonishing miracles occurred right before my eyes, including a lame man who walked for the first time in his life. I'd had a revelation of who God is – and it gave me confidence to believe his word as never before.

6. Persistence

Being a Christian is not a path to a life without difficulties. Frankly, any teaching that even suggests 'problem-free' living is unreal and verging on dishonest. There is no get-out clause in the Bible that exempts Christians from going through storms. The truth is that most miracles happen during challenging times. I once heard

Reinhard Bonnke say, 'Breakthrough only happens when you're embattled.' He was talking from his own experience of living in the miraculous – reaching millions of lost people.

In a storm, you have two options.

First, you can decide to go back into the safety of the harbour and postpone the journey until a better day. The problem is that there never is a better day than today to make your journey. Even if the water seems calm at first, this can be deceptive, as storms can come suddenly and unpredictably. So procrastination is actually one of the biggest barriers to reaching your God-given destiny and seeing the miraculous.

Secondly, you can choose to stay on course and battle through the stormy waters. It's scary at times, and often you'll hear critics around you 'advising' you that it's unwise to continue. But if you persist, walking on the word of God, you will get through – emerging with remarkable stories of God's miraculous protection and provision in your life.

The key to experiencing the miraculous is to keep walking on the word long enough – both in the good times and in the challenging times. Persistent faith in God's word is what is required if more miracles are to be experienced.

Down – But Not Out

With each step he took, Peter got closer to Jesus. This really was a remarkable feat – a truly historical moment. For the first time ever, a human being walked on water. But suddenly, in a split second, Peter made a critical mistake. He became distracted. Instead of looking towards Jesus, he focused on the storm. It might have been just a quick glance at first but it was a crucial error. The sight of the storm overwhelmed him. The reality of the howling winds and the raging seas became too much for him. Daunted and frightened by circumstances, Peter panicked, at which point he immediately sank beneath the waves, almost disappearing from sight.

But Peter's voice could still be heard calling out, 'Lord, save me!' Right away, Jesus was there for him. He pulled Peter out of the water and gently spoke to him, saying, 'You of little faith – why did you doubt?' This was not a harsh rebuke – far from it. I can imagine Jesus smiling as he spoke to Peter. It was as if Jesus was saying, 'You were doing so well, Peter – in fact, you could have carried on if you'd kept your focus on me.' I once heard someone preach on this incident, ending his sermon with the words, 'The conclusion of this story is that Peter sank. Amen.' Not exactly an encouraging conclusion – is it? To merely summarize the incident with the thought that Peter sank really does miss the point. Yes, Peter sank – but he didn't drown!

Whatever the circumstances around you, it is imperative that you keep walking on what God has said. It is the one foundation that is strong enough to withstand any storm that comes your way. Sometimes when you're walking through a storm it doesn't feel as though a miracle is happening. It's only when you look back and see how perilous it was that you understand God was taking care of you, seeing to it that you weren't consumed. It was he who miraculously brought you through, even though you were not aware of this when you were going through it. Keep walking on God's word. It is without doubt the thing that will carry you and ultimately see you through. Remember that when God tells you something, it must come to pass even if the circumstances of life seem to militate against it.

The worst mistake we can make in our pursuit of the miraculous is to lose sight of Christ. Only when this happened did Peter's body succumb to the raging seas around him. Yet before, when his eyes were firmly fixed on his Lord, there was no possibility of that happening. Why did Peter sink? He became distracted. This is one of the most dangerous things that can happen in our pursuit of the purpose of God. Sometimes, even seemingly genuine things can cause us to waver in our vision. But if we are going to experience more of the miraculous, we must keep our eyes firmly focused on Jesus, 'the author and perfecter of our faith' (Heb. 12:2). He, after all, is the miracle-worker.

4

LESS IS THE KEY TO MORE

There's an old saying that 'less is more'. It was coined by the architect and furniture designer Ludwig Mies van der Rohe, one of the founders of modern architecture and a proponent of simplicity of style. The phrase denotes the idea that creating space to focus on one object will have a more striking effect than complicating it with many. Hence people today talk about being 'minimalist'. And so it ought to be the case with us, especially when it comes to moving in the miraculous. Isaiah 28:10 says, 'For precept must be upon precept, precept upon precept, line upon line, line upon line, here a little, there a little' (NKJV). In God's economy, less really is more.

I love music, and studied piano at the School of Music in Belfast. Although I rarely perform in public now, there's nothing more enjoyable for me than to sit down at the piano and play. It's stress-relieving, relaxing and uplifting. The best music, in my view, is the simplest. Take Pachelbel's 'Canon in D major', for example. This is a variation on a theme that's soothing, uncomplicated and one of the most popular classical pieces in the world, often heard at weddings. People love it because they can understand it. It builds up slowly. The listener can discern what's going on. With each new variation, it's quite easy to tell the slight change that is occurring. That's what makes it so good. It's not a sudden splurge of musical notes, but uncluttered and simple.

De-cluttering

The truth is that if we are going to see a greater manifestation of the miraculous, it's not a complicated rush of activity we need. Instead there has to be a willingness to create space for God to do what only he can do. Remember, most miracles aren't just stumbled upon – they happen because of readiness and because room has been made for them to occur. Often our lack of leeway makes it difficult for us to move with the Spirit.

So what exactly will it take for the twenty-first-century church to see more miracles? Is it really about putting on more programmes? No. Some churches have so much going on it's as if they've programmed God out of the proceedings.

Far from putting on a variety of extra programmes, 'less' is what we need to learn. It's about making space for God to manifest himself to us. This requires a tidying-up process on our part, de-cluttering many of our existing activities and reassessing whether they are helpful or in the way.

Many churches are far too reluctant to clear the clutter, for fear of what might be exposed. They don't always verbalize their concerns, but they wonder: will people still worship without our style of music? Will members keep coming to church if the programme changes? Will they continue to give financially if we stop the activities that we feel we should end? Of course there's nothing intrinsically wrong with music, programmes, activities and the rest. But if those things become more important than God himself, they turn into clutter. If they are an obstacle to miracles happening, they are surplus to requirements and so need to be cleared out of the way.

The process of de-cluttering is not about losing out but about providing opportunities for God to pour in. Only when there is emptiness can God really do something of significance. Instead, many churches feel that the best way to initiate momentum is by packing out each week with a list of options so that members can be engaged and get involved. They have much going on, but when all is said and done the question must be asked, 'What is being achieved?' Remember, moving in the supernatural isn't so much about creating momentum as about making space for a moment of divine encounter.

The Starting Point of a Miracle

Interestingly, the first recorded miracle of Jesus was at a wedding, in the town of Cana in Galilee. Disaster was looming for the party organizers because they had run out of wine. The six huge jars were completely drained. But unbeknown to them that day, it was the perfect condition for a miracle. Emptiness is always a good place to start when you want to see the supernatural. What should have been a terrible anti-climax was soon to turn into an even more joyful occasion.

Jesus ordered that the empty vats be filled with water. It can be very easy to underestimate the courage of the servants who poured. They surely must have wondered why they were doing such a strange thing, since the winemaking process takes many weeks to complete and does not involve pouring water first. But whatever they thought, they got on with doing what he had told them. What happened next required even more courage. Jesus instructed that some of the liquid be drawn out of a jar and given immediately to the master of the banquet. Precisely when the water turned to wine is something we don't know. The Bible doesn't tell us, but I have a sneaky suspicion it was transformed at the very last moment, perhaps just as it was picked up by the wine tester. It certainly wouldn't surprise me if it did happen like that.

Isn't this the way God so often works, leaving it to the final second? Whichever way it occurred, the master of the banquet drank the wine, not realizing that a miracle had just taken place, and he was astounded by its quality. He complimented the bride and groom, saying, 'Everyone brings out the choice wine first and then the cheaper wine after the guests have had too much to drink; but you have saved the best till now' (John 2:10). What had been a crisis of emptiness was turned by Jesus into a miracle of fullness. And it wasn't just any old wine but the very finest. God can turn things round in a single moment. But getting us to create space for it to happen – well, that's another matter altogether. Making room for the miraculous is about being willing to be emptied of our own plans, submitting to God's instead.

There are times in life when we come up against seemingly impossible situations that require us to throw ourselves entirely into his hands. Only when that happens do we really allow God to miraculously turn things round. But so often, the need to feel we're in control prevents us from letting go, and instead we call in every expert under the sun to advise us on what alternative course of action we might take. If some Christians had been among the stewards at the wedding party in Cana, they would have vehemently disagreed with the ludicrous idea of pouring water first, preferring instead to try something very different. But much as they might have tried, nothing else would have worked. Wine can't be rushed. The day would have ended in disappointment and a miracle would never have happened.

Sensitivity to God's Voice

Making room for the miraculous is not about adding lots of things into the mix in the hope that one of them will work. It's really about taking lots of unnecessary things out so that we can give God some space to work as only he can. We must create the right atmosphere in our lives if we're going to clear the way for the supernatural to occur. That's about learning sensitivity to what God is saying and following it up with faith and obedience. These two things always work side by side. God often leads us to say and do things that don't necessarily make sense. Nevertheless, as Mary advised the wedding servants, just 'do whatever he tells you'.

Baggage

There is a new realm of the miraculous that every Christian can enter into. In Revelation 3, God spoke to the church at Philadelphia and told them he had set before them an 'open door'. The thing is, when God opens the door, no one can shut it – not even the Devil. Yet many Christians never get to move through it and into the next level. Why is that? It's because of the baggage they're carrying on their backs. There's so much of it that it stops them getting through. Their desire to move on isn't the issue. Their hunger to see more miracles is not in question. But what they're carrying is the very thing that is holding them back. The 'open door' isn't wide enough for the baggage to get through, because it's been deliberately designed that way.

When I travel, I like to take as little luggage as possible. My wife, however, is the opposite, preferring to take as much as she possibly can. She will get everything into her suitcase that can be fitted in. I'm sure she'd even include the kitchen sink if she could. I once asked her, 'Why do you take so much?' Her reply echoes that of millions of women around the world: 'Just in case I need it.'

But in God's economy, our journey into the supernatural requires as little luggage as possible. God wants us to create room so we can see more of his wonders, and the only way that space can be created is if we have the courage to leave some things behind.

Before I left Ireland to study in England, I bought myself a very good digital piano to bring with me. I loved it, and would practise on it for hours each day. It was my pride and joy. One day, I felt the Holy Spirit challenged me to give it away. It wasn't through an audible voice but with a gentle prompting in my spirit. I must confess I was not particularly pleased at the prospect of doing such a thing, even though I knew it was the right thing to do. I thought, 'There's no point in preaching about faith if I'm not prepared to practise it myself.' I actually felt God showed me who I was to give it to. So I called the couple concerned and told them what I intended to do. The same day, I arranged to deliver the digital piano to their home. When I arrived I was met with overwhelming expressions of gratitude and appreciation which included tears of joy, laughter, smiles, shouts and then more tears. The couple kept saying, 'Thank you, Roy. This is going to be such a huge help as we learn to play the piano.' To be honest, at first I really couldn't bring myself to be happy. The only tears coming to my eyes were the ones that appear when you feel the pain of something you've lost. But it wasn't too long before all that changed. I can't fully explain why, but I became euphoric, delighted to have done what God had asked of me. The loss of what was precious to me didn't compare to the joy of giving it away. The Bible does say, 'It is more blessed to give than to receive' (Acts 20:35).

As I sat at home that evening, I heard a noise at the front door. I thought nothing of it, but curiosity got the better of me and I looked to see if someone was there. Beneath the letter box was an envelope. I opened it and found inside a cheque from someone who has always been a great source of encouragement. They wanted to bless me, and the amount on it was more than double what I had paid for the digital piano that I'd just given away. As I stood there, I heard the Holy Spirit speak into my spirit, saying, 'I dare you to trust me. I dare you to trust me.' I realized what God was teaching me. It wasn't wrong for me to have a digital piano, but I had to learn to obey him and not to hold on to anything, instead giving it away at God's say-so. It was about creating space for God to display his glory. For a moment, it felt like I'd lost out. But there's no such thing as losing when you act in obedience. Even if I'd never received the cheque, I would still have been blessed. Money isn't the issue. The heart is.

Moving On

And so it is for those who want to see more miracles. There must be willingness to move on, leaving behind what's really not needed. We can't live our lives as hoarders. Things that were yesterday's joys can become today's rubbish. Yet there's something about the human psyche that wants to store the past, feeling it might become valuable again one day. Even things that were once precious can be held on to unnecessarily, becoming obstacles to future progress. Many Christians spend their days telling stories of what happened in a bygone era. But this is a new day. Yesterday's blessings were for yesterday. God has miracles in store for us that we have not yet seen. The only way they will happen is if we make room to receive them. Leaving some things behind isn't about sacrificing – it's about creating room to receive.

God can do more in one instant than we could ever attempt in ten lifetimes. Making space for him to manifest his presence is the preparation we need for those miraculous moments that are yet to come. It's at times like this that one encounter with God can lead to situations being transformed for ever. But the process of de-cluttering takes a step of faith and not a little courage, as there are sometimes periods of seeming inaction. There can even be occasions when it appears that heaven has gone silent. Some make the mistake of assuming the sense of nothingness means it's not working and so revert to endless programmes again. But we shouldn't be afraid of silence. Why be threatened by quietness? 'In quietness and confidence shall be your strength' (Isa. 30:15 KJV). God is watching over his word, and in his good time he will bring it to pass. We just need to keep our lives clear of clutter so that nothing will hinder him working in and through us. Remember, the moment for a miracle will come, so always be on the ready for it.

The prophet Elijah was depressed and discouraged. This was the man who had brought about breathtaking miracles in his ministry. He'd even seen the dead raised. Yet in a season of silence, when his life was under threat, he felt deserted and lonely. How ironic that the man who saw others brought back to life wanted to die himself (1 Kgs 19:4). In the midst of his deep sorrow, he felt the effects of a powerful wind. But God wasn't there. Then he saw an earthquake, and after that a raging fire. Strangely, in all the places you might expect to find him, God wasn't to be found. Then suddenly, Elijah heard from God in a way that many might not expect him to speak – a 'gentle whisper'. It was in the calmness and spaciousness of a moment that God ministered to Elijah, preparing him for the next stage of his journey and the greater miracles that were to come.

One of the secrets of moving in the miraculous is realizing that less is more. It's not so much about 'doing' as about 'becoming', giving God room to minister into your life so that he can use you to fulfil his purpose and channel his supernatural power through you in the process.

5

IN PURSUIT OF THE MIRACULOUS

My favourite television show is *The Apprentice*. Each week, a group of ambitious young professionals is split into two teams and given various products to sell. They must then go out and make as much money as they possibly can in the time limit they're given. The winning team (i.e. the one that earns the highest amount) is given a luxury prize, while the losing team must re-enter the boardroom, where one of them is fired.

The boardroom battles are often the most fascinating part of the programme. Professional business people must really identify with some of the manoeuvrings that go on there, seeing it on an almost daily basis for themselves. Time and again, it's every man and woman for themselves. More often than not, friendships and loyalty are left outside the door as each contestant is utterly ruthless in their attempt to stay in, even at the expense of their team-mates. When someone has serious ambition, they will do almost anything to win. Being ruthless really is the aim of the game.

But in our pursuit of the miraculous, we need to have a different kind of ruthlessness. It's not about selfish gain and personal ambition. In God's eyes, these are characteristics of pride, the very thing that comes before a fall (Prov. 16:18). The type of ruthlessness we need is an unwillingness to settle for anything less than what the Bible says. It's about making sure we remove all personal hindrances that can block us from seeing what we know God desires. Often, there's a frustration in the hearts of people who have a hunger to move in the miraculous. This can even be misunderstood by some. But that dissatisfaction is created by God. He won't allow us to be content just where we are. There are more miracles yet to be experienced. There are manifestations of his glory that we have not yet seen. God is longing to work in us and through us, and the only way we are going to get there is if we become uncomfortable with the status quo. We will never change the future if we don't disturb the present.

Disabling the Enemy

The book of Judges is a ruthless account of God's people at war, not to be read by the faint-hearted. It paints a picture of what happened when his people obeyed him – and of the consequences when they didn't. In Judges 1:1–8, the tribe of Judah engage in conflict with the Canaanites. We're told that 'the Lord gave the Canaanites and Perizzites into their hands' (Judg. 1:4). However, when the king of the Canaanites (Adoni-Bezek) was caught, they didn't kill him – instead they cut off his thumbs and big toes. This was a symbolic statement, signalling that they had disabled the enemy, rendering him harmless as a warrior. The thumbs are crucial to making the hands work. Without thumbs it is impossible to fight. The big toes are crucial to making the feet work. Without them it is impossible to flee. By removing the thumbs and big toes, they cut off their enemy's ability to fight and flee – so he could never be a threat to them again.

In our desire to move in the miraculous, we must be ruthless in removing the power of those things that prevent us from seeing what God wants for us. Hebrews 12:1 encourages us to 'throw off everything that hinders'. Removing barriers isn't a negative process, or at least it doesn't have to be. For every negative, there's always a positive. For each weakness, there's a strength. So it's a matter of dealing with the things that can block us from seeing the miraculous by looking at the appropriate alternative. Let's think about some of those hindrances that need to be disabled.

Disabling Doubt

Doubt usually comes in the form of a deceitful question spoken in the guise of a friendly voice. Its real intention is to plant seeds of confusion in your head, questioning what you're doing and why you're doing it. When doubt strikes, it usually asks, 'Are you sure about this?' or 'What if this goes wrong?' and sometimes it's heard to ask, 'What will people think?' Remember, this was the very tactic that the serpent used in the Garden of Eden to question God's original command that Adam and Eve should not touch the tree of knowledge or eat from it. But the serpent asked temptingly, 'Has God said?' and they yielded to doubt.

I will never forget preaching at a small church with around seventy people one Sunday morning. The service was so boring it was demoralizing. I was even fed up myself, and I was the preacher! Afterwards, I called people out to receive prayer for healing. In the line of people there was a man in a wheelchair. He hadn't walked for many years because of an illness he'd contracted. So I went down to him first and asked, 'Do you believe that God can heal you?' He replied enthusiastically, 'I do!' His response startled me. I continued, 'If I pull you from the wheelchair, will you come?' His answer was witty, but faith-filled: 'Well, I guess I wouldn't have any choice, would I?' So I pulled him up, but as I did so a thought suddenly resonated round my mind: 'What if this goes wrong?' For a moment, my confidence was severely rattled. It sounded like a reasonable enough thought but it was actually a major attack of doubt. It had the effect of destabilizing me, trying to convince me not to go any further because it would lead to embarrassment and failure. However, I'd started and so I determined to stay with it, even though everything in my mind was telling me to help the man back into his wheelchair as he wasn't going to get healed.

I remember turning in the opposite direction, so that my back was towards the man as he leaned precariously onto me. I took his hands and said, 'Let's walk.' It was the moment of truth. Either he would be healed or he would stumble into me and together we would fall flat on our faces. After a few footsteps, I was encouraged that his hands were still in mine – unless his arms had left their sockets and were just dangling to the ground . . . Thankfully, though, that wasn't the case. We made our way right round the auditorium – and for the first time in years he walked. After that, I asked the man to walk on his own – and that's exactly what he began to do, slowly at first but eventually at a normal walking pace. I put the wheelchair on the platform to let the people see what had happened. Besides, the man didn't need it any more and was very happy to walk home without it. Word spread round the community about the miracle that had occurred in the church that morning, and in the evening service there were more than three hundred people present, very unusual for that church, but all because they'd heard about the miracle.

Don't give in to doubt. Instead, be ruthless in cutting off its ability to fight and flee. Remember, Jesus said that if we have faith and 'do not doubt', we can see to it that every mountain that's in the way is removed. Perhaps doubt is your mountain. Well, by faith, let's get it moved.

Disabling Indecisiveness

'A double-minded man,' says James 1:8, is 'unstable in all his ways.' Double-mindedness is what you get when you spend too much time pondering whether or not to do what God is telling you – sometimes saying yes and other times saying no. Such a way of life leads to instability and insecurity. God would rather you be hot or even cold. But lukewarmness he detests, and 'spits' out of his mouth (Rev. 3:16). Either get on with it, or get out of the way. Don't spend years trying to decide. As J.John says, 'There is only enough time to do the will of God.'

The wise man who built his house on the rock is like someone who hears God's word and puts it into practice. The foolish man who built on sand is like someone who hears God's word but doesn't build on it, opting to go elsewhere. The storm came, and the strength of the foundations was exposed: the wise man's house stood firm, but the non-solid foundation of the foolish man's home meant it was unable to withstand.

If God has plotted a course for your life, stay with it and refrain from deviating. Don't believe in a God of miracles one day and then question it the next. This is symptomatic of a wrong approach to the Christian life that says, 'If God doesn't speak to me now, I won't believe him.' Instead, just keep building on what God has already said to you. Don't be constantly on the lookout for fleeces, like Gideon in Judges 6. God is not obliged to respond to demands for signs like this. Sometimes he does, but most of the time he doesn't. The truth is, when God speaks, he doesn't need to repeat himself. Remember, his word is the most vital component of any miracle. So it's a matter of listening and believing. Romans 10:17 tells us that faith comes by hearing the word of God. Make sure you disable the power of unstable thoughts over your life. Have the courage to build on the word of God. Decisiveness is the way to ruthlessly unhinge the grip of double-mindedness.

Disabling Pride

Pride is a major barrier that hinders many from experiencing the miraculous. Symptoms of pride are things like self-centredness, selfishness, self-sufficiency and, sadly, self-delusion. Pride is intrinsically linked to a wrong perception of personal importance which in turn leads to deception and ultimately sin. For example, it was pride that caused the prodigal son to demand his inheritance before it was his time – and the rest, as they say, is history.

Humility is of course the very opposite. It's not about being perfect, but being willing to be vulnerable enough to admit it when you get it wrong. Interestingly, James makes it clear that confession of sin can even lead to supernatural healing (Jas 5:16). The moment a deceitful thought is confessed and brought into the light, the power of the deception is broken – its thumbs and big toes cut off, so to speak. God then finds it easy to minister to a person like this.

I'm not a fan of ministers' meetings. At one ministers' business conference I attended a number of years ago, I felt frustrated as I listened to various people making their points of order and arguing their case. But in a moment, everything changed. One of the church leaders present, a well-known preacher, stood up and asked if he could say something that wasn't in line with the current topic of debate. In front of four hundred of his colleagues, he publicly apologized to another minister about whom he had spoken disparagingly at a different conference. The other minister, who was also present, came forward to the stage and there they embraced and wept. The meeting had been rather noisy before, but now there was a reverent silence. The man who had been wronged then got onto his knees, and with tears began to wash the feet of the other minister. There was an atmosphere of complete brokenness and humility that day. Even the most hardened of hearts was melted. A wise old pastor stood up afterwards and observed that where there is humility and brokenness, God can bring healing, signs and wonders.

In pursuing the miraculous, there is no room for pride. In fact, we have to be ruthless with it. It is inevitable that there will be times when we get it wrong and make mistakes. That's why accountable relationships are so vitally important – where we can be asked tough questions by people who love and believe in us. This is how we can cut off the thumbs and big toes of pride – it's called humility.

Disabling Disobedience

The pitfall we need to avoid when we talk about obedience is legalism – a way of thinking that believes it is possible to earn God's favour merely by doing good works. This really isn't what it's about. The true outworking of a life completely surrendered to God is a desire to obey him out of love and devotion, not rules and regulations. Jesus once said, 'If you love me, you will obey what I command' (John 14:15). He himself led by example, subjecting himself to God the Father, saying, 'I do exactly what my father has commanded me' (John 14:31). A little later, Jesus went on to say, 'If you remain in me and my words remain in you, ask whatever you wish, and it will be given you' (John 15:7).

'Remaining' in this context denotes the idea of obedience and submission. Being a Christian is not like a hard-labour prison sentence. Far from it: it's to do with using our God-given freedom to recognize Christ's authority and Lordship – and making it our delight to submit to him. It's as we do this that our will comes into subjection to God's will, the two becoming one, and on that basis, anything we ask for is not out of selfish motives or personal advancement but a desire to see the will of God come to pass.

Blatant disobedience, however, is a blockage to the miraculous, i.e. wilfully doing something that you know is not pleasing to God. Many miracles have never happened because of this very reason. The only way it can be dealt with is by ruthlessly cutting off its ability to fight against you and flee from you. Three words sum up how you can do this – surrendering to God.

On one occasion in Matthew 8:5–13, a centurion (in charge of 100 Roman soldiers) came to Jesus and informed him that his servant was at home, sick and paralysed. Jesus offered to go to his home to heal him, but the centurion respectfully declined. This wasn't out of rudeness or inhospitality – he'd got a revelation that most people before him had never received. He explained, 'Lord, I do not deserve to have you come under my roof. But just say the word, and my servant will be healed.' As if that wasn't enough, the centurion went on to explain, 'I myself am a man under authority, with soldiers under me. I tell this one, "Go," and he goes; and that one, "Come," and he comes. I say to my servant, "Do this," and he does it.' By saying this, the centurion was explicitly recognizing the authority of Christ and his word, and was letting it be known that he was more than willing to surrender to it. Jesus was 'astonished', and at his command – 'Go! It will be done just as you believed it would' – the servant was healed that very hour. It was obedience and surrender that led to the miracle.

Disobedience in its most simple definition is a lack of submission to the authority of God. It's an enemy of all the amazing miracles God wants to manifest in your life – and as such, its thumbs and big toes need to be ruthlessly removed. Submitting to God is the key.

Disabling Negativity

Faith by its very essence is positive, not negative. It believes for possibilities instead of focusing on problems. A confession of faith is thus one of positivism – not negativism. The truth is that negativity is a breeding ground for unbelief. Hebrews 12:1 talks about 'the sin that so easily entangles'. It can be easy to get tangled up in chains that hinder us from seeing the miraculous – one of them being negative thoughts and words that lead to unbelief, the 'sin' to which Hebrews 12:1 refers.

Amazingly, after experiencing the miracle of the parting of the sea and deliverance from the Egyptians, some of the children of Israel began to grumble. Have you ever noticed what happens when a few negative people get together? Their negativism can spread infectiously, pandering to an age-old human tendency to focus on what's wrong instead of celebrating what's gone right. Some of God's people even began to look back through rose-tinted spectacles to the past, wishing they'd stayed in Egypt (Exod. 16:3). Think about it: God had miraculously saved their lives, delivering them from terrible bondage, and all some could do was moan and complain – even having a go at Moses, the man of God who'd led them to freedom. Looking back to the good old days is always a huge mistake. Usually, those 'good old days' weren't nearly as wonderful as they're made out to be. But negativity does tend to have a blind perspective – identifying problems but offering no solutions.

Not long after, the complaining attitude of many of the children of Israel became even more serious. While Moses was on the mountain receiving the law, they grew impatient, and the grumbling became worse. Someone had a clever idea. Why not make an idol using gold from jewellery worn by the two-million-strong community? So they made a golden calf and worshipped it as God. Now this would have been at most only a few weeks after the miraculous parting of the sea, which shows just how quickly negativity can raise its ugly head. When Moses returned, 'his anger burned' (Exod. 32:19) and he destroyed the golden calf, ground it to powder, mixed it with water and made the children of Israel drink it. Ruthless? Absolutely, but Moses was not willing to let negativism contaminate the people of God.

Many of us struggle to be positive at times, especially when we're tired and weary or when things haven't worked out quite as we wanted them to. But it's in times like this that we must show complete and utter ruthlessness in cutting off the thumbs and big toes of negativity.

The way to do that is to develop a strong and genuine optimism that's determined to celebrate the miraculous, both what we have experienced in the past and the hope of what's yet to come. That's what faith is all about.

Disabling Bitterness

When I first launched out in ministry, I had lots of enthusiasm and excitement. Sometimes I was perhaps a bit naïve in the way I went about ministering – but I'm convinced God likes passion, as long as the heart is pure. I was also honoured to have friends around me who believed in me enough to let me get it wrong from time to time – yet they'd still encourage me to keep going for it.

On one occasion, however, a minister who I didn't know very well let me know that he thought I was a hopeless case. I was told that I might as well quit the ministry, as he felt I didn't have what it took to do anything of significance, and would probably do more harm than good if I stayed. Those words cut into my heart like a knife. Although I didn't show it outwardly at the time, I was deeply hurt. It was a surprise to me to feel like that, as I'm not the sort of person who easily takes offence. But the hurt grew. It festered so much that it turned into anger and eventually into bitterness. I thought, 'How dare he say that to me?' It was my first thought in the morning and my last thought at night. For a period of time, my ministry became focused on proving that minister wrong. It really wasn't right and it was undoubtedly becoming a hindrance.

Around that time, I received an invitation to minister in America. My hosts said, 'You get yourself out here, and we'll look after you.' A few days later, I received a windfall of £200 through the post. I was so happy, as this would cover the cost of my air fare. It all sounded too good to be true – and it was. Suddenly, I clearly heard God speak to me, not audibly, but quietly in my heart. God said, 'Give the one who offended you half the windfall money.' I tried to reason with God, 'Lord, I need this money to take my flight to America,' but deep in my heart I knew it was the right thing to do.

So I wrote a cheque for £100. That doesn't sound like much, but it was to me because I didn't have much money. I sent it off and blessed the person who'd offended me. I then realized what was happening. God wanted me to be ruthless in getting rid of the bitterness in my heart, cutting off its thumbs and big toes. It was a blockage – and it needed to be removed. Once I'd released it, it never came back.

A few days later, as I was on the verge of cancelling my trip to America for lack of money, I received my mail. I opened the first letter and was humbled by what I read. It was from a church in Belfast, the Malvern Assembly, where I grew up. A few days ago, they'd felt God challenge them to send me a gift to support my ministry – and they sent through a cheque for £1,000! As I sat there and held the gift in my hand, I cried – amazed at how God works. Then I heard a familiar voice speaking in my heart: 'You see, you could have kept what you had in your hand – or you can have what I have in mine.'

Don't let bitterness and anger hold sway over your life. Cut them off ruthlessly – even if it means you lose out in the short term. In the long term, you will create the opportunity to see more miracles than ever before. That's a fact!

Ruthless Pursuit

Seeing more of the miraculous really does require a ruthless pursuit. It's not about attaining perfection but about removing hindrances and being obedient. By cutting off the thumbs and big toes of the Canaanite king in Judges 1, the tribe of Judah had defeated the power of the enemy. Interestingly, though, the rest of the book of Judges recounts what happened when God's people became lax and didn't show the kind of ruthlessness that God wanted. As a result, wars were lost and defeat was inevitable.

As we maintain a ruthless momentum and keep a sense of audacity to believe that the greatest miracles are still before us, we will not be disappointed. When we do what we can, God does what we can't.

6

THE MIRACULOUS POWER OF THE PROPHETIC

There are three things that every person who moves in the miraculous needs to have: hindsight, insight and foresight.

Hindsight is an understanding of what has already gone before us. We do well to learn from people whom God has used to work miracles in the past, observing their strengths and learning from their struggles too. James 5:17 recalls the prophet Elijah, referring to him as 'a man just like us'. Time and again, history teaches us that God uses ordinary people to do extraordinary things.

Insight comes from being thoroughly steeped in the Bible. The danger if this is not the case is that we live off experience alone. But personal experience must always be checked and balanced by the word of God. The scriptures are our basis of faith. This is the very thing that produces true faith, for 'faith comes by hearing the word of God'.

Foresight sees what's ahead. As well as learning from the past, there needs to be a vision of what God wants to do today and in the future. After all, surely the greatest miracles are yet to come.

It's the third 'sight' that this chapter focuses on – fore-sight.

Here are some statements that were accepted as true at the time they were made – but later proven to be very wrong:

'Man will never reach the moon, regardless of all future scientific advances.' Dr Lee De Forest, father of radio and grandfather of television.

'This "telephone" has too many shortcomings to be seriously considered as a means of communication. The device is inherently of no value to us.' Western Union internal memo, 1876.

'I'm just glad it'll be Clark Gable who falls on his face, not Gary Cooper.' Gary Cooper on his decision not to take the leading role in *Gone With The Wind.*

'We don't like their sound, and guitar music is on the way out.' Decca Recording Company rejecting The Beatles, 1962.

'Aeroplanes are interesting toys but of no military value.' Marshal Ferdinand Foch, Professor of Strategy, France.

They just didn't see it, did they? And that's the point.

In a sense, hindsight is easy. It's a great luxury to be able to look behind us and see what has already happened in history. But it is all too easy to sneer at the doubters and sceptics whose predictions were way off the mark. And don't forget, most doubting voices are a reflection of popular opinion at the time. The truth is that the majority of us would have been among those doubters too.

Foresight

Foresight is quite another thing. It's about living above see-level. Prophecy is a positive declaration of the future based on what we view by faith. However, it doesn't deny present realities – to pretend that problems don't exist is simply unreal and actually lacks integrity. But it believes for the best despite current circumstances. There is always hope in the heart of a person of true belief. Even if the miracle they believe for seems a million miles way, they know that it's just a matter of time before they get there. No circumstance is too difficult for God. Nor is there any problem that is too much for him. No matter how high and wide the mountain may seem, faith will always rise up, gaining God's perspective and seeing that there's a way ahead.

Romans 4:17 gives us a great insight into how God works. God always finishes before he starts, calling 'things that are not as though they were'. He is the alpha and the omega, the beginning and the end. God knows the outcome of every situation we're faced with. He's in your tomorrow while you're in today. So with the eye of faith and a little bit of prophetic foresight, we can see beyond what is currently happening and determine not just to face the facts, but to faith the facts. What an amazing thing it is to know that God really is in control.

Before Jesus came to the earth, died on the cross and rose again from the dead, God had already settled the final solution for sin. This is why Jesus is referred to as 'the Lamb that was slain from the creation of the world' (Rev. 13:8). God, who works from a place of completion, knows the end from the beginning. He had made miraculous provision for human depravity even before the fall. Then in the Old Testament, lambs were slain to bring atonement for guilt, types and shadows prophesying what was predestined to come, namely that Christ (the Lamb of God) would atone for the sin of the entire world.

How did people in the Old Testament receive the miracle of salvation? By faith, just like us. The difference between then and now is a matter of perspective. We look back to the cross, but they looked forward. We see what has already happened, but they saw by faith what was yet to come. In one sense, they required even more faith than us. The life of Jesus is today a historical reality, written about, documented and widely accepted as true. But they didn't have that advantage. This makes Isaiah's famous 'suffering servant' prophecy (Isaiah 53) all the more miraculous. He had a revelation which summed up the life of Christ hundreds of years before it actually happened. That's true prophetic foresight.

God, the Master Architect

The role of an architect is to visualize and design a structure. It's their job to see what it will look like before anybody else does. Of course today, with all our amazing computer technology, architects find it much easier to communicate how a potential building will appear using cinema-style graphics. I have attended a number of building presentations and been amazed at how precise and detailed the architect's visual images have been. But God is the master architect. He knows what the final picture of life looks like. His greatest desire for us is simply that we believe him, even though we haven't physically seen the final outcome with our eyes.

Believing in God isn't about mere mathematical probability. It's not about looking for some clinical form of scientific acceptance of his existence, even though the arguments for this outweigh those against. It's that we may know him and be involved in his purpose for the future. This requires a truly believing heart. Yet, contrary to many sermons that have been preached over the years, faith is *not* spelt R.I.S.K. It makes for a great soundbite – but it's as wrong as wrong can be. Risk would imply the possibility of failure, but God is incapable of this. He has seen the final result – and it is good.

Declaring it Before it Happens

Take Gideon, for example: one of my favourite Old Testament characters, mainly because he is the unlikeliest of heroes. The first thing God said to him was that he was a 'mighty warrior'. But at that moment, Gideon looked anything but a great man of valour. Even so, God declared who he was before he became it. After Gideon had made many excuses and requests for signs of confirmation (which God graciously granted), God proceeded to whittle down his army from thirty-two thousand to ten thousand and then to just three hundred men. Imagine that: an army of three hundred led by Gideon going up against the might of the Midianites and the Amalekites, who had tens of thousands of highly trained soldiers led by powerful generals. Doesn't look too promising, does it? But the size of an army doesn't matter so much to God as faith does. You see, God declared to Gideon that the battle was won before it was even fought. He said to him, 'Go down against the camp, for I have delivered it into your hand' (Judg. 7:9 NKJV). In the end, Gideon's little army didn't even have to fight. They simply split off into three groups of 100 round the fringes of the enemy's camp and, at the signal, blew their trumpets and smashed their jars. It seems a rather ludicrous way to attack your enemy – but what happened next was simply breathtaking. The enemies, startled by the blast of trumpets and crashing of jars, presumed a much larger force was attacking. So in the confusion of the moment, they began to fight each other as Gideon's men stood and watched. It was a victory that was nothing short of a miracle.

Why did it happen in such an absurd way? Surly God could have arranged for Gideon and his men to march gallantly into the enemy's camp and fight the battle of their lives, emerging as victorious warriors? But it didn't happen like that, because God was showing his people that only he could have done this. The truth is he didn't even need as many as three hundred men. The battle already belonged to the Lord. In effect, it was he who fought and won it, not Gideon. All God wanted was belief in his purpose – and people who dare to see by faith are true warriors in his eyes. When a miracle happens, people will always look on and observe, 'Only God could have done that.' But the miraculous victory over the enemy wasn't the real issue for God. That was the easy bit. Convincing his people to see that he had already won was quite another matter. And nothing much has changed, even in the twenty-first-century church. Today, God is still looking for people who see that the victory has already been won at the cross and then live in it for themselves, making it an everyday reality to experience the miraculous.

The Father of the Faithful

Abraham was another man who experienced more than his fair share of the miraculous. But as with Gideon, God often declared what would happen before it actually occurred. On one occasion, he told Abraham to prepare to be a dad again – and not only that, he would be the 'father of many nations' (Gen. 17:4). There's nothing strange about that, on the face of it at least. But Abraham had a problem. He was 99 years old and his wife wasn't too far behind at 90! He fell on his face and laughed. But his laughter was not based in unbelief or sarcasm. He understood that when God says something it must come to pass, no matter how unattainable it might seem. It was medically and physically impossible for Sarah to bear a child, but nine months later the miracle was born. Romans 4:16–21 refers to the faith of Abraham:

> Therefore, the promise comes by faith, so that it may be by grace and may be guaranteed to all Abraham's offspring – not only to those who are of the law but also to those who are of the faith of Abraham. He is the father of us all. As it is written: 'I have made you a father of many nations.' He is our father in the sight of God, in whom he believed – the God who gives life to the dead and calls things that are not as though they were. Against all hope, Abraham in hope believed and so became the father of many nations, just as it had been said to him, 'So shall your offspring be.' Without weakening in his faith, he faced the fact that his body was as good as dead – since he was about a hundred years old – and that Sarah's womb was also dead. Yet he did not waver through unbelief regarding the promise of God, but was strengthened in his faith and gave glory to God, being fully persuaded that God had power to do what he had promised.

Say What You See

In the year 2000, I prayed with a young couple who'd been told by doctors that they could not have children. They came broken and devastated because they so desperately wanted children. As I prayed, I saw in my spirit that God was going to do a miracle. I quoted the words of Isaiah 54:1, 'Sing, O barren woman, you who never bore a child; burst into song, shout for joy.' As I did that, I could sense faith rising in their hearts more than it ever had before. I felt inspired to speak out what I saw and prophesied that they would have a child. A few weeks later, I was delighted to get word that the couple were expecting a baby. Nine months on, their little boy was born – an extraordinary miracle since they had been told it was medically impossible. But if you don't see it before you see it, you'll never see it.

No Worries

One of the most dramatic miracles in the ministry of Jesus was the raising of Lazarus from the dead. The build-up to this amazing incident is one of strange calmness on Jesus' part, almost to the point of what might appear to be a lack of concern. He was in no rush to get to Lazarus' home even though he knew that he was very sick. At one point, Jesus said to his disciples that Lazarus was merely 'asleep'. But they didn't see what he was really saying, thinking this meant Lazarus was recovering from his illness, whereas Jesus was actually referring to his temporary death.

When Jesus finally arrived at the family home, it seemed too late, as Lazarus was already dead and buried. Martha, the sister of the deceased man, immediately expressed her distress and frustration at Jesus' apparent delay. She said, 'Lord, if you had been here, my brother would not have died' (John 11:21). But Jesus knew exactly what he was going to do. He knew this was not the end of the story. The purpose of everything that was about to unfold that day was 'so that God's Son may be glorified through it' (John 11:4). Interestingly, it's in the midst of all the grief that the shortest verse of the

Bible appears: 'Jesus wept.' Why? Certainly out of compassion for a family who were mourning, but also because of people's inability to see his purpose and the blatant, even antagonistic unbelief of the Pharisees, who had tried to stone him just a few days earlier despite having seen him do incredible miracles.

Jesus told the men around him to 'remove the stone'. What a nail-biting moment this was for those standing by. Could the unthinkable really happen? Was it truly possible for a dead man whose body had already been wrapped in grave cloths and buried to rise from the tomb? These were probably the thoughts of the people watching. But for Jesus, it was already a foregone conclusion. All he declared was, 'Lazarus, come out,' and the dead man had no choice but to stand up and come forward. If Jesus had not prefixed the words 'Come out' with the name 'Lazarus', then it's likely that everyone who had ever died would have come forward, such is the power of his word. Jesus had already seen what was about to happen before it even happened. That's why he didn't have to worry.

Being Certain of What We Haven't Seen

Moving in the realm of the miraculous requires us to see God's purpose in our hearts before we see it fulfilled with our eyes. The great 'hall of faith' in Hebrews 11 is full of people who saw by faith. It is worth noting that the chapter begins with these words: 'Faith is being sure of what we hope for and certain of what we do not see.' How can we be certain of what we do not yet see? After all, conventional wisdom says that 'seeing is believing'. But this is not the case as far as God is concerned. Remember, if you don't see it before you see it, you'll never see it.

Jean-François Blondin was a brilliant nineteenth-century French acrobat famous for crossing the gorge below Niagara Falls on a tightrope 335 metres long and 50 metres above the water. He used a number of different theatrical variations in his act. There is a story that he once asked the thousands of people waiting to see him perform, 'Do you believe I can do this?' The crowd shouted back, 'Yes!' He posed the question again: 'But do you really believe it?' The hysterical crowd replied all the louder, 'Yes!' Then he offered to carry any volunteer across on his back, but his invitation was met with a deafening silence: no one was prepared to do it. The only person willing to be carried across was his manager: he knew Blondin, knew what he was capable of, and trusted him.

They set off, the man on Blondin's back, and reached the other side safely. People clapped their hands and cheered, mesmerized by Blondin's brilliance and astounded by the manager's courage. But he knew he had nothing to worry about, because he had complete faith in Blondin, knowing he hadn't failed yet and convinced that he never would. This is surely an example of what faith really is. It's trusting God because of who he is. When you know the faithfulness of our heavenly Father, you know that his promises are absolutely true, and that whatever happens, he will not let you down. That's was 'seeing' is really all about.

Here are six ways in which prophetic foresight that sees the miracle before it actually happens is outworked:

1. Prophetic foresight prepares today for what will happen tomorrow

When you know you've got an appointment, you need to plan ahead, arranging where the meeting will be, how you're going to get there, when you're going to arrive and what you need to bring with you. It's the same with a miracle. When you see it in your heart, you still have to be thoroughly prepared for a journey towards destiny. But prophetic foresight isn't enough in itself. Proper preparation is extremely important: without it we can miss the very thing we've seen in our heart. We mustn't become lax in our prayer life and in Bible-reading. On the contrary, these things are as essential as ever.

2. *Prophetic foresight speaks the language of 'when', not 'if'*

'If' implies a possibility of things not working out. But someone who sees a miracle by faith doesn't talk about 'if' – instead they look forward to 'when'. There is something definite and certain about faith that sees what God's purpose is before it physically comes to pass. After all, it is being 'sure of what we hope for'. 'Hope' in this context is not merely wishing for the best but looking forward with optimism to what we know is ahead. When you are certain that God has made a promise, you can be assured that it's just a matter of time before it is fulfilled. Pondering 'if' is often a sign of unbelief.

3. *Prophetic foresight is confident of the future*

There is no need to be anxious when you know that God is ultimately in control. Nor is there any reason to be insecure and concerned about what others might be thinking or saying on your way to a miracle. Faith that sees isn't worried about how you're going to get through difficult circumstances. Instead, you know that God's got it all in hand.

A characteristic of confidence is peace. I was once on a plane that had just taken off from Seattle airport on its way to the east coast of America. The aircraft had barely got off the ground when suddenly it began to dive back down. There was panic as passengers expected a horrible crash. Yet amazingly, even though I'm not a lover of flying, I was completely at peace. You see, I was on Kingdom business and I was absolutely sure that God was going to get me there. The plane was eventually brought under control and landed safely. When God has a plan for your life, you shall not die until it is completed.

4. Prophetic foresight lives with courage and conviction

Most people are short-sighted. Their focus is on current needs. Never mind the future: they want to know how to get through today. There is little understanding of what faith is all about. Instead they're driven by needs. However, those who move in the miraculous are not motivated merely by what's currently happening but by vision of what is to come. They see with eyes of faith and are determined to pursue what they know and believe is true. Pressing on towards the goal takes courage and conviction, especially when the voices of those who don't see it grow louder and more critical. It's at times like these that persistence is crucial. Don't be tossed around by tides of opinion. Andrew Evans, General Superintendent of the Australian Assemblies of God and founder of the Family First Party, once said, 'The secret of success is to keep doing the right thing long enough.' No matter what, just keep saying what you see.

5. Prophetic foresight stays on track, despite life's twists and turns

Bumps are to be expected along the journey. Remember the story that Jesus told about the two pathways. One was wide and appealing but its destination was destruction. The other was narrow and winding, but at the end of it paradise awaited. The dream that God places in your heart must always be at the forefront of your thoughts. It's this that makes every footstep along the way worthwhile. When you lose sight of it, that's when you're tempted to give up. A blurred vision asks, 'What's the point of going on?' especially during those uphill struggles that require extra effort. Don't lose sight of the miracle – stay focused. You will get there.

6. Prophetic foresight grasps the big picture

Wrong perspective has led many a person to miss their miracle. Instead of seeing the big picture, they become transfixed by one aspect of it. The secret to gaining God's perspective is to stand back for a while and look at the canvas long enough from a distance. Then you'll begin to understand the outline of what he is doing. Seeing that helps you understand why he then focuses bit by bit on various aspects of his purpose, bringing the whole thing together in his good time. As when you're doing a jigsaw puzzle with a thousand pieces, it always helps to know beforehand what each piece is contributing to.

It's as Good as Done!

Prophetic foresight is often a prerequisite for a miracle. It involves seeing it in your heart before viewing it with your eyes. With faith like this, you can laugh in the face of impossibilities, knowing already what the outcome is. Whatever your situation, don't lift up your eyes to the need but say, like David, 'I lift up my eyes to the hills – where does my help come from? My help comes from the LORD, the Maker of heaven and earth' (Ps. 121:1–2). In another passage, God said of his people, 'Before they call, I will answer' (Isa. 65:24). This is the mark of a work that has already been completed.

Walt Disney died shortly before the unveiling of a new section of Disneyland. At the opening ceremony, the compère for the evening called his widow Lillian to come forward and lead a tribute to the great man. As she approached the stage, he commented sympathetically 'It's just a pity Walt didn't see all this.' Lillian Disney took the microphone and immediately corrected him, pointing out, 'He did see it.' You see, Walt had already seen it before anyone else. That's the reason why they were there in the first place.

There are three basic components to a miracle: 98 per cent is the word of God, 1 per cent is faith and 1 per cent is obedience. Put those three things together, and they constitute an irresistible force making it well nigh impossible for miracles not to happen. God has said it, so make sure you see it. Remember, if you don't see it before you see it, you'll never see it!

7

ATTITUDE DETERMINES ALTITUDE

'She thought, "if I just touch his clothes, I will be healed"' (Mark 5:28).

The people who inspire me most in life are those who battle against the odds and win. I love the audacity of people like Edmund Hillary, whose determination to be the first to conquer Everest meant he refused to quit even when it seemed he would never achieve his dream. After one failed attempt, Hillary turned to the as yet unconquered mountain, with his men listening behind him, and said, 'Mount Everest, I'll defeat you yet. You're as big as you're going to get, but I'm still growing.' It wasn't long afterwards that he finally achieved his goal of being the first to get to the top of the world's tallest mountain.

Of course the Bible is full of inspirational stories of people who dared to believe they could triumph even when it seemed they were looking disaster in the face. The ultimate example of this is Jesus Christ, who even though suffering a humiliating death on the cross went on to defeat sin and the works of the Devil, even beating death by rising again from the grave.

One in a Crowd

Among the many less well-known Bible characters who experienced the impossible was a woman in Mark 5:24–34 whose name we don't even know. Everything was against her. To begin with, she had a bleeding condition, and in those days women like this were considered unclean and left on the fringes of society. She'd searched for a medical cure over a long period of time but never found it, spending all her money in the process. In Mark 5, she's just one woman in 'a large crowd'. She is on the fringe of the masses, lonely, desperate, bankrupt and very sick. Yet out of all those thousands of people, why was she singled out? After all, she wasn't any more important than anyone else, nor did she hold a position of significance. And there's something else that may come as a surprise – it wasn't her need for healing that made her stand out. Think about it: in a crowd of many thousands of people who are there to see Jesus the miracle-worker, there would undoubtedly have been some desperately needy people, some in even greater need than this woman. So why her? What was it about this woman that caught the Holy Spirit's attention? The answer to this can be summed up in two words: faith attitude.

Even though she was in a seemingly impossible predicament, she had a 'thought' that would literally change her life. Her 'thought' was that if she could push her way through the crowd and just touch Jesus once, she would be healed. Was this a reasonable thought? Probably not, as there was a big crowd, likely to have been unruly and disorderly. So the idea of getting from the fringes to the centre was a bit crazy. And besides, reason would conclude that there was little or no chance of her being healed, even if she did manage to touch him. But the woman's 'thought' was birthed in faith, not reason. She had a faith attitude – a belief that with God, absolutely nothing was impossible.

Attitude

If you are to be the type of Christian who experiences the miraculous in your life, then like this unnamed woman you need to have the right kind of attitude. I once heard a little saying which I think contains an important message: 'Attitude determines altitude.' Your attitude as a Christian will determine how high you're going to fly.

There are some wrong attitudes that make it really difficult for us to rise into the realm of the miraculous:

A negative attitude

Focusing only on the problems and not the possibilities is very unhelpful for anyone who has a desire to move in the miraculous. It really is a mistake to exalt difficult circumstances above God instead of lifting him above our challenges. Too often, we can be daunted by the severity of what's happening around us instead of seeing how God can bring us through.

A complaining attitude

Instead of turning frustrations into positive action, the complainer just moans all the time. This is another huge hindrance to seeing miracles. Complainers are very good at identifying what has gone wrong but fail to offer solutions so it can be put right. What often happens is that complaining attitudes feed off each other. That's why many complainers tend to go around in groups. But this doesn't help us in our journey to see more of the miraculous.

An angry attitude

People are sometimes bitter at past disappointments, even from years ago. If the resentment isn't dealt with, it grows and festers, becoming a dominating factor in a person's life. Anger contaminates faith. An important key for anyone who desires to move in the miraculous is to understand that before you sow in faith, you must make sure you remove any weed from your seed, otherwise it will kill the effectiveness of your faith. Bitterness is one of the biggest contaminators of all.

An arrogant attitude

If we lack humility and are unwilling to submit to others it is another huge hindrance to moving in the supernatural. Even Jesus, the ultimate miracle-worker, submitted himself, being baptized by John the Baptist in order to 'fulfil all righteousness'. If a submissive attitude was good enough for him, it's good enough for us.

A cynical attitude

Speaking in a sarcastic tone, saying things like 'Prove it to me,' is not the kind of attitude that's conducive to seeing more miracles. For example, when Herod wanted to see Jesus perform some kind of miracle (Luke 23:8), his motive was cynical, as if Jesus were an entertainer who could perform tricks and illusions. Jesus is not interested in impressing people. He simply doesn't need to. It's people with serious faith attitude he is really looking for, that is to say those who trust in who he is.

An unbelieving attitude

We do well never to forget that God promised the children of Israel that they would inherit the 'promised land'. Yet the promise was clearly not appropriated, as the Bible tells us that it was 'unbelief' that prevented a whole generation from entering it (Heb. 3:19). An unbelieving attitude is a major barrier to experiencing the miraculous.

But the unnamed woman in Mark 5 had the right attitude. She knew what would happen if she pushed through. Herein lies a crucial lesson. Experiencing the miraculous isn't just about knowing the possibilities in our minds. At some point, we need to act according to our convictions. As she stood on the fringes of that massive crowd in desperation and financial ruin, she realized that this could be her one and only opportunity to receive a miracle. So she made the most of it and began her long journey towards Jesus.

Make Your Mind Up

How many times have we not experienced the miraculous because we've missed our opportunity? Often in life there comes a make-or-break moment when we are challenged to put into practice what we know in our mind to be true. It is wrong to assume that opportunities like this will come our way again and again. This is why we ought to make the most of every opportunity and go with the courage of our conviction. That's exactly what the woman did in Mark 5. She put her faith attitude into practice and acted accordingly.

In January 2004, I appeared on a Christian television chat show in London as a guest. My fellow guest was a

Pakistani pastor whom I had never met before. After we'd finished the programme we had some coffee together, and during the course of our conversation he asked me, 'Will you come and preach the Gospel in Pakistan?' I gave him the answer Christians typically give when they really don't want to do something – 'I'll pray about it.' So I went home that night, and didn't think about it again: I had a dismissive attitude, believing the increased militancy in Pakistan made it too dangerous to go there.

Three years later, in January 2007, I was in my office when a call came through to let me know that the Pakistani pastor was passing by. I was asked if I would like to meet him for coffee and I said 'Yes' enthusiastically, having forgotten our previous conversation. As we sat and chatted, out of the blue he asked me again: 'Will you come and preach the Gospel in Pakistan?' Again I said, 'I'll pray about it.' However, his response was not what I was expecting. 'I thought you might say that,' he said, 'but I want you to know that I have already prayed about it and I've come with the answer. God has told me to tell you that you must go.' When I heard this I nearly choked on the chocolate digestive biscuit that I had just dunked in a hot cup of coffee. The little pastor stood at the door of the office and would not allow me to leave until I gave him dates when I would travel to his beloved nation. So I pencilled in 6–13 November 2007, thinking in the back of my mind that this would give me eleven months in which to convince God to change his mind and send someone else. But then I realized what was happening. I'd had the opportunity once before and God was graciously giving me another chance, I think the last chance, otherwise he would use someone else to go.

Eventually, November came. Just two days before I travelled out, the news headlines were full of stories of political turmoil in Pakistan. The country was placed under martial law and large gatherings of people were banned, which seemed to put in jeopardy the four-day outreach event at which I was meant to speak. I made the journey out there anyway, feeling very nervous since I was well and truly out of my comfort zone. On my first evening there, I met with two important government officials. At the start of the meeting, they made it clear to me that our meetings would not be allowed to go ahead. However, as I explained why I had come to Pakistan, God gave miraculous favour. One government minister said, 'Okay, your meetings can go ahead.' The other man, a senior security official, said, 'Please be assured that I will personally provide your security throughout your time in Pakistan.'

So we went ahead with our four-day outreach event, and many thousands of people attended. On the third night, I was asked to pray for people to be healed. Since I couldn't go down and lay my hands on the people, because of a concern about the possible presence of militants, I pronounced a prayer of healing over the huge gathering from the platform. Suddenly, in the midst of my prayer, a voice cried out, 'I'm healed! I'm healed!' The pastors who were on the stage with me beckoned the woman forward, one telling me that she was an influential lady in that city. She came to the microphone and recounted that for five years she'd suffered painful facial paralysis due to an illness she had contracted. It was so severe that she could hardly speak, slurring her words at an agonizingly slow pace. But when the prayer of healing was pronounced the paralysis immediately ceased, the pain left and she could speak normally again. 'I'm healed! I'm healed!' she shouted again, clearly a very happy woman. The people gave a massive cheer that must have been heard some distance away.

A few days later, as I stood in the airport waiting to catch my flight back to London, the senior official who had provided my security came to see me. He took me to one side and said, 'Roy, thank you for coming to Pakistan. By the way, I thought I had better let you know that the woman who was healed of facial paralysis just a few nights ago is my wife. I also felt it would be good to inform you that the following evening, I too gave my life to Jesus.' Astounded and amazed, I got onto the plane back to the UK, utterly dumbfounded at what had happened. But I was humbled by the thought that a dismissive attitude on my part could have denied me the honour of experiencing astonishing miracles like this – and many more besides.

Pushing Through

Imagine what it must have felt like for the unnamed woman in Mark 5 as she began to move through the crowd. It must have taken enormous courage for her to do that. Of course, anything in life that's worth pursuing takes courage. As she pushed her way towards Jesus, she must have encountered some sceptical voices saying things like, 'Who do you think you are?' 'You'll never make it,' 'Just give up now, he's not interested in you.' When you have the courage to embark on a journey towards an experience of the miraculous, you will often encounter discouraging voices that give you all the reasons why you shouldn't go any farther. Sometimes those voices are motivated by blatant cynicism and unbelief. But more often than not, they are genuine people who think they're saying the right thing, for your benefit. But like the woman in Mark 5, we need to have a single-minded faith attitude that simply refuses to go back to the fringes. No matter what anybody said to her, she was certain that with just one touch of Jesus' cloak, she would never be the same again. That's what her motivation was.

Here are some characteristics of this attitude:

A faith attitude says: God says it and I believe it

This is the kind of attitude that God loves to work with. That's why an old Yorkshire preacher called Smith Wigglesworth moved so prolifically in the miraculous. It wasn't because he was any cleverer than anyone else. It was simply because he had a serious faith attitude. He once famously said, 'God said it. I believe it. That settles it.' Moving in the miraculous requires a childlike faith that really believes what God says in his word is true. When I was a kid, my dad used to play a game where he'd put me on the first step of the staircase and say, 'Jump.' So I'd jump, knowing he would catch me. Then he would put me on the second step and say, 'Jump.' So I jumped again because I knew I could trust him. Then the third and the fourth and right up to the fifth. Each time he said 'Jump,' I simply took my dad at his word because I always knew he would be there to catch me. A faith attitude simply jumps when God our heavenly Father says so – and expects him to do what only he can do. A faith attitude says: All things are possible

People who experience the miraculous in their lives are those who believe for the best in the midst of the worst. They know deep in their hearts that all things are possible with God. So even when they come up against problems the size of mountains, they know that all it takes is faith as small as a mustard seed to see circumstances transformed from negative to positive. Instead of focusing on the scale of the challenge, they 'fix their eyes on Jesus' (Heb. 12:2), with whom nothing is impossible. That's why it is so important for us to grow in deeper revelation of who God is. The scale of your upward vision determines the scope of your outward vision. So let's see God for who he is – and then we'll get his perspective on our challenges and see them as they really are.

A faith attitude says: I will listen to God more than to people

Of course it's important to take sound advice and make ourselves accountable to a few people who are close to us. But there's an old saying that 'too many cooks spoil the broth'. It's possible to have so many people speaking into our lives that confusion sets in because of the diversity of the opinions expressed. Everybody's got an opinion. For every 'Yes' there will always be a 'No'. For every 'Go' there will always be a 'Stay'. For every encouraging word there will always be a discouraging word. Better to receive one fresh word from God for yourself than to listen to the views of many people. It's the word of God that sustains you and acts as the foundation on which you can build to see more of the miraculous.

A faith attitude says: I will not quit when I feel discouraged

There are no Bible promises that exempt us from feeling discouraged at times. When you have a dream in your heart to experience a miracle, there can often be frustrations and discouragements because of the seeming lack of progress towards what you're believing for. What's even worse is when you feel you're regressing – as if the very thing you've been trusting for is moving farther out of sight instead of getting more within reach. But it's in times like this that a real faith attitude must shine through. It's very easy to trust God when there's lots of money in the bank and life is generally going well. But the shield of faith is most needed in the midst of warfare – when the fiery darts of the enemy are coming in your direction. Keep trusting because your miracle is not far away.

A faith attitude says: With God, I can overcome

The language of defeat and doom doesn't feature in the vocabulary of people of faith. This is not to suggest that such people don't have trials and testings like any normal human being. But whatever obstacle they face, they are convinced that with God's help they can succeed. Remember, you can't be an overcomer unless you have something to overcome. The greatest miracles are experienced by those who look impossibilities in the face and declare that the problem will be turned into a testimony to what God can do.

A faith attitude says: God is on my side

Paul the apostle once said, 'If God is for us, who can be against us?' (Rom. 8:31). It is possible to lose this important perspective in our pursuit of the miraculous. In times of warfare, we can have an exaggerated picture of the enemy, seeing him as bigger than he really is. It's important to remember that God is on your side. He simply wants you to believe him. That's why God sometimes allows us to go through challenging circumstances – so we can really learn to trust him. Perhaps the Devil has tried to plot a course for your downfall. But God can take what has been meant for bad and turn it right around for your good. You and God are always a majority. All he is looking for is trust, for you to know that anything he does for you is with your best interests at heart.

A faith attitude says: The best is yet to come

Optimism and hope are characteristics of people with a faith attitude. This is not about superficiality and denial of realities. Faith in God is not some delusional form of false positivism. Nothing could be farther from the truth. It is about understanding that God works from a place of completion. He knows the end from the beginning. He sees the final picture. The outcome has already been decided, because through his death and resurrection Jesus Christ has defeated sin, death and the works of the Devil. So whatever happens in this life, in Christ all is well because the victory has already been won. This is the very basis of why Christians can believe in the miraculous.

The Impossible Becomes Possible

The story of the unnamed woman who pushed through the crowd in Mark 5 is a prophetic picture of what happens when people with faith attitude stay true to their convictions. She is a shining example of someone who dared to believe in the possibilities of what God could do. Instead of remaining on the fringes she progressed towards the centre. After all, that's where Jesus was. She wasn't prepared to wait on the outskirts in the hope that Jesus might pass by. True faith leaves nothing to chance. So she pursued him instead. Even though the journey was tough and at times unbearably uncomfortable, the goal was surely worth every footstep.

It's so easy for the twenty-first-century church to remain on the fringes, never pushing through to experience the miraculous. Having assessed the risks, lots of churches have concluded that the journey isn't worth it. Concerns about reputation and respectability rule the day. So they opt instead for a hassle-free life. Sadly, that kind of attitude will never see a breakthrough in the miraculous. But the woman in Mark 5 wasn't like that, and her faith clearly paid off. After a long and arduous trek through a mass of desperate people, she eventually got within touching distance of Jesus. Stretching out her hand as far as she could to clasp hold of his cloak, she finally touched him and 'immediately . . . she was freed from her suffering'. After years of discouragements, bankruptcy and humiliation, just one touch and her health was transformed back to wholeness. She was never going to be the same after that. She'd received a miracle.

Who Touched Me?

After touching Jesus and receiving complete healing, the woman discreetly tried to make her way back into the crowd. But there's no such thing as a discreet miracle. You can't return to the fringes after a miraculous experience like this. Jesus always notices faith, and this occasion was no exception. He stopped everything, asking, 'Who touched me?' Given that no one else in the crowd had realized what had just taken place, it's not unreasonable to imagine a sense of bewilderment among the disciples. Their sentiments were, 'Lord, there are lots of people touching you. This is a big crowd, after all.' But Jesus insisted on finding out who had done it. Many people had tried to get Jesus' attention that day but one had shown true faith, the kind of belief that gets real results. And Jesus knew it.

Determined to find out who this mystery person was, Jesus persisted until she finally came forward. The Bible says she 'fell at his feet'. This one statement tells us everything we need to know about the unnamed woman. Her faith wasn't merely rooted in what Jesus could do but in who Jesus was. She recognized him as the Son of God, and falling at his feet was her act of worship, a sign of deep respect and reverence. Jesus affirmed her by saying, 'Your faith has healed you.' The word 'healed' here is the Greek word *sozo* – meaning released, saved, delivered, freed, transformed. It was the woman's persistence that led to this.

Press On

The reality is that your faith can make a difference. Moving in the miraculous means pushing through every opinion and circumstance we encounter. A faith attitude refuses to give up and turn round. Convinced that just one touch of Jesus will transform circumstances for ever, it persists and presses on until it's close enough to lay hold of him. That's the kind of serious faith attitude which is going to see miracles happen.

8

BREAKING THROUGH

Jesus once declared, 'If anyone says to this mountain, "Go, throw yourself into the sea," and does not doubt in his heart but believes that what he says will happen, it will be done for him' (Mark 11:23). This verse comes just after Jesus had cursed a fig tree that bore no fruit. The disciples were astonished at how quickly the tree had withered after his pronouncement. It is highly likely that Jesus did this to provoke them to see what can happen in response to words spoken in faith. It certainly adds a new light to Proverbs 18:21, which says, 'The tongue has the power of life and death.' Jesus encouraged his disciples, 'Have faith in God.'

On another occasion, recorded in Luke 17:5–6, the disciples said to Jesus, 'Increase our faith.' Jesus replied, 'If you have faith as small as a mustard seed, you can say to this mulberry tree, "Be uprooted and planted in the sea," and it will obey you.'

Both these passages show us the immense possibilities of faith. There really is nothing that is impossible with God. The problem for so many people who are in need of a miracle is that they focus on the size of the need instead of the power of God. Merely seeing the scale of the mountain leads to feelings of inadequacy and consequently to inaction. This misguided thinking results in defeatism and resignation. It really is the very opposite of what Jesus taught in the two passages mentioned. All it takes is for someone to have faith the size of a mustard seed, and circumstances can be changed beyond recognition. Have you ever seen a mustard seed? I have. It's a tiny object, a speck in the palm of your hand. That's how much faith can make a difference and cause a miraculous breakthrough.

In this chapter we'll look at some keys to understanding the requirements of breakthrough faith that will unlock the door to the realm of even greater miracles.

1. Breaking Through Requires *Us* to Move

Faith that sees a miraculous breakthrough doesn't merely wait for God to move. It seems such a waste of time to spend hours in prayer asking God to do all the work, as if he hasn't been moving and now he ought to make a start. This really does miss the point of the Spirit's work.

One of the ways the Bible pictures the Holy Spirit is as wind. For example, in John 3:8 Jesus says the work of the Spirit is like the wind, noting, 'You hear its sound, but you cannot tell where it comes from or where it is going.' On the day of Pentecost there was a sound 'like the blowing of a violent wind' (Acts 2:2), confirmation of the coming of the Holy Spirit.

What is wind? The simplest way to define it is 'air in motion'. This is like the Holy Spirit, always moving. There is never a time when the Spirit is not at work. This really does call into question prayers such as, 'Lord, will you move?' Asking this is like asking fire to be hot, or water to be wet, or wind to blow. These things just happen – because God is always on the move.

I once heard about a preacher who was walking in the valleys of South Wales. On his trek, he stopped to pray. There was no one else around, so he decided he would pray aloud. He cried out to God with a booming voice, 'Will you move?' Suddenly, in the distance, he heard God speak to him through the echo of his very own words, turning the question back to him: 'Will you move?' While so many Christians are busy asking God to work, God is actually asking them to do something. While we expect God to move, we must remember that he expects us to move too.

People who have breakthrough faith understand that God is always in motion. So they learn to go with the Holy Spirit. That's what real breakthrough is all about: simply agreeing with and following the Holy Spirit, so that 'whatever you bind on earth will be bound in heaven and whatever you loose on earth will be loosed in heaven' (Matt. 16:19).

2. Breaking Through Requires Us to Keep Trusting What God Says

In Matthew 8, Jesus told his disciples to cross to the other side of the lake, so they climbed into a boat and set off across the water. On the way, a furious storm suddenly broke out. Understandably, the disciples (some of whom were experienced fishermen who knew what could happen in ferocious storms) were fearful for their lives, since water was getting into their boat. They tried desperately to keep afloat, but seemingly to no effect. Yet in the midst of all their efforts to stay alive, they noticed something that frustrated them beyond belief. Jesus was sleeping. They quickly woke him, saying, 'Lord, save us! We're going to drown!' However, Jesus' response was hardly encouraging: 'You of little faith, why are you so afraid?' Perhaps a bit harsh, don't you think?

Jesus then rebuked the storm. Mark's account tells us what he said: 'Quiet! Be still!' (Mark 4:39). The wind died down, the sea became calm and everything was peaceful again. The disciples were amazed. They knew Jesus could heal people. They had seen him drive out demons. But now they wondered among themselves, 'Who is this? Even the winds and the waves obey him!' (Mark 4:41).

But why did Jesus rebuke his disciples so harshly during the storm? Surely it was reasonable for them to feel afraid? On this occasion, was it not understandable that their faith should falter? Did they not have some right to be frustrated that he was sleeping? Well, not as far as Jesus was concerned. We do well to remember what had already happened in Matthew 8 up to that point. Jesus had healed a man with leprosy by the power of his word. He healed a centurion's servant with his word. Then the multitudes came to him – and he healed them, as well as driving out evil spirits with 'a word' (Matt. 8:16). It was with the same powerful word that he had told the disciples they were to cross the lake, and so they should have trusted him. That is why Jesus rebuked them for their unbelief in the midst of the storm. 'From everyone who has been given much, much will be demanded' (Luke 12:48).

When God speaks, he expects us not only to listen to what he says but to trust him too. After all, his word is by far the largest component of any miracle. Some miracles involve deliverance from circumstances, but others occur by God bringing us through the storm. Both require faith in God's word. This is the type of breakthrough faith that trusts in God – whatever is going on around.

3. Breaking Through Requires Us to See Beyond Present Circumstances

I'll never forget hearing the story of a woman who came for prayer at a church where I was speaking. She was struggling with sickness. But even though her prognosis was not good, she felt she had a word from God that she would be healed. So she anticipated receiving healing, even looking forward to telling her doctors about it when it happened. She was among the line of people who responded to my invitation to come forward for prayer for healing, and when I reached her I began to pray. I had hardly got into my prayer when suddenly she interrupted me, saying, 'That's it. Yes, that's it. I'm healed. Thank you, Jesus!' Imagine that – someone getting healed before I'd even had a chance to get through my anointed prayer! I love it when that happens.

The following week, she went to see her doctor. Just as she had anticipated, she said, 'I've come to let you know that I've been healed.' He was somewhat startled by such a strong statement, probably thinking she'd gone mad, but he agreed to do more tests. On seeing the results, the doctor was amazed to confirm that there was no sign of disease in her body.

4. Breaking Through Requires Us to Launch Out Into the Deep

In Luke 5, Simon and his team had been fishing all night and returned in the morning feeling disappointed at not having caught anything. Tired and weary, they were happy enough to oblige when Jesus asked if he could use one of their boats as a makeshift platform so he could speak to the crowd gathered before him. However,

Simon was clearly taken aback when Jesus, having finished teaching the people, said, 'Launch out into the deep and let down your nets for a catch' (Luke 5:4, NKJV). At first, there was a touch of resistance on Simon's part. Having worked hard the night before, what was the point in going out to sea again? The hassle, the stress, the work involved: surely it was all too much? But Simon must have thought, 'As crazy as this seems, what have I got to lose?' So he dared to trust Jesus' word and launched out as he'd been told. To say that he got more than he bargained for is a major understatement. They caught so many fish that their little boat couldn't contain them, almost sinking under the strain. They even had to get help from others, using every available boat to carry the massive catch back to shore.

So often, people never experience the miraculous because they don't launch out into the deep when God tells them to. Remember, God's word is often inconvenient. He tells us to do things that sometimes don't make a lot of sense. We can either respond, 'It's not worth the hassle, so I won't go,' or, as Simon did, 'Because you say so, I will let down the nets.' But the results of launching out and letting down our nets at God's say-so are always worth any hassle. Simon's catch was truly miraculous. The fish must have been competing with each other to be caught that day!

I 'launched out into the deep' as an evangelist in 1998. At the time, it was a major step of faith for me. I'd had opportunities to be involved in roles in other churches and ministries, some of them offering good salaries. But I knew I had to say, 'No thanks,' because none of them was what I was called to do. There came a point when I literally had no openings and it seemed as if any dreams of serving as an evangelist were dead in the water, so to speak. But I kept believing, and as I did that, God himself opened doors for me to function in my calling. Miracle after miracle happened as a result of faith that broke through. There were miracles in terms of ministry opportunities, provision of finances and most importantly of all, many people coming to faith in Jesus at events I led. The truth is, if I'd never launched out into the deep and had opted instead to stay in the security of a role I was never called to do, I would have missed so many amazing opportunities to witness the power of God with my own eyes. Breakthrough faith dares to launch out into the deep and let down the nets at God's word.

5. Breaking Through Requires Persistence

Sometimes miracles happen instantly. Other times they occur gradually. In the case of something developing slowly over a period of time, persistence is much needed. This is a major challenge for the church today. We live in a quick-fix 'convenience' culture that demands results now. But some miracles just don't happen like that. Why is that? Often this is because the work that God does in us before we receive the miracle is even more important than the miracle itself.

It's like the process of seed developing into fruit. The seed must first be planted in the ground. Then there is slow and unseen growth. On the surface nothing seems to be happening. But under the soil a lot is going on. Life is growing. It takes weeks, even months. Then out of the ground the shoots of life appear. It's agonizingly slow, but the process can't be hurried. It is only through a process of patient planting and steady growth that the fruit eventually forms and grows. Even then, there is the temptation to pull it from the branch and eat it too soon.

But this would be a mistake, as it's not ripened yet. It needs time and persistence, just like breakthrough faith.

In John 9:1–12, the blind man did not receive an instant miracle. Jesus went through a strange routine of spitting on the ground, mixing his saliva with the roadside dust and rubbing it into the man's eyes. In all the artistic impressions I've seen of the miracles of Jesus on stained-glass windows in great churches and cathedrals, I have not yet come across a portrayal of this incident. Spitting isn't exactly a glamorous way of healing people, and I have certainly never heard of someone operating under a spitting anointing!

After rubbing the clay into the blind man's eyes, Jesus commanded him to go and wash in the Pool of Siloam. Exactly how far that was from where the blind man was, we don't know. Some suggest it was more than a day's journey. So what was happening? Jesus explained even before he started the healing process, 'This happened so that the work of God might be displayed in his life' (John 9:3). There was more going on than just the miracle. Jesus was making a wider point. People had assumed the man had been confined to a life of misery because he was under some kind of generational curse due to the sins of his ancestors. But Jesus was actually using the man to manifest his miraculous glory. He was demonstrating that he had the authority to break the power of the past and create new life. The healing of the blind man was in fact a creative miracle – and it certainly provoked a response from all who knew him.

If your miracle is still in seed form, this is a crucial time for you. Remember, the Devil finds it easier to kill a seed than to fight a harvest. Perhaps on your journey to the miraculous, God is doing more in you than you realize. Be persistent. God often does more behind your back than he does in front of your eyes. Faith that experiences a breakthrough is persistent.

6. Breaking Through Requires Your Heart to Believe When Your Mind Wonders

In the armour of God described in Ephesians 6, faith is likened to a shield. Its purpose is to protect us from the fiery darts of the enemy. The worst thing that can happen when someone is embarking on a journey towards a miracle is that they stop trusting God. The moment this happens, they become exposed to anything and everything the Devil has in his arsenal of weaponry. Discouragement, despondency, disappointment, disillusionment and lots more besides will come flying in their direction – and because the shield is down, they'll all make direct hits.

When I first began to move in the miraculous, the more I saw, the more I grew in confidence. One night, I was speaking at a jam-packed church in South Yorkshire. After preaching, I called people to come forward for prayer for healing. One woman who responded was suffering with spondylitis. She wore a surgical collar and was in a wheelchair, unable to move much because of the severe pain in her neck and back. As I prayed, I was so sure God was going to heal this woman that I removed the collar from her neck and pulled her out of the wheelchair. After a few minutes of prayer, something happened in my mind that gave me a crisis of confidence. It looked to me as if the woman was getting worse, not better. So I quickly finished my prayer and put her back into her wheelchair. Her head seemed to sink and I was sure her skin had turned yellow.

I prayed quickly for the remaining few people, and as soon as I'd said goodbye to the minister of the church I got into my car and left. I felt totally dejected, beyond what words could describe. It was as if someone had kicked the confidence out of me. On the way home, I made a decision that from that point on I would not pray for people, convinced that somehow I'd done more harm than good to the woman in the wheelchair. So for around six months I didn't pray for anybody and reverted to being only a speaker.

Then one day, out of the blue, the leader of that same church in South Yorkshire called me and asked if I would come back and preach there again. At first, I tried to make my excuses but he insisted I come. So I booked a date about six months after I'd last been there. The evening of the event finally came, and as I walked into the auditorium I was dreading what people might be saying, since I was so sure something awful had happened to the woman in the wheelchair. One thing was sure in my mind: I would not be praying for anybody that night.

As I sat on the front row before the service began, a woman came over to me and said, 'Hi, Roy. Do you remember me?' I genuinely didn't recognize her. She said, 'You prayed for me when you were last here. Remember, you removed the collar from my neck and even pulled me out of the wheelchair and then helped me back into it.' As she spoke, she had my full attention! She said, 'Afterwards, I just sat there for a while longer, even after you'd left to go home. But something amazing happened shortly afterwards. I felt the power of God moving all over my body. Again, I got up out of the wheelchair and the pain that had partially gone this time completely eased. So for the past six months, I've not needed the wheelchair or the collar because I've been healed!' When I heard this, I was speechless – probably a miracle in itself. What was even more amazing was when she said to me, 'Thank you for trusting God all this time for my healing.' I thought, 'If only you knew.' Then I heard a gentle voice speaking into my spirit, saying, 'Why did you stop trusting me?'

Your heart must keep trusting when your mind wonders. Don't give up – ever. Remember, faith is like a shield – it's there to protect you. God is working, whether we realize it or not. Stay on the right path and you will see a breakthrough.

God's Word

Seeing and experiencing more of the miraculous is undoubtedly an audacious adventure. But breaking through in the realm of the miraculous doesn't always happen as quickly as we might like. That's where faith comes into action, trusting God to lead the way. God gave Joshua instructions to march his army round the walls of Jericho for seven days. On the seventh day, they were to circle the city seven times, with seven priests blowing their trumpets, and then the people were to shout aloud. So that's exactly what happened. Interestingly, the number seven has significance in the Bible, symbolizing perfection – in this instance, God's perfect timing. So after the seventh march on the seventh day, Joshua commanded the people, 'Shout! For the LORD has given you the city!' (Josh. 6:16). As they cried out, the walls of Jericho came tumbling down and the city was taken by Joshua and his army. Breakthrough happened and victory was sweet.

One word from God is all it takes to make a difference in your circumstances. One whisper from the Holy Spirit can cause barriers to be demolished. One blast of God's voice can destroy the chains of sickness and oppression over a person's life. And remember, the word of God in your mouth is as powerful as the word of God in God's mouth. One word is all it takes, and walls can be broken down. Breaking through to a miracle is all about trusting in what God says, agreeing that his will shall be done 'on earth as it is in heaven'.

9

SOME MIRACLES ARE BIRTHED

Life is fast, and getting faster. Can you imagine what it would be like without the Internet, emails and mobile phones? The truth is we're so dependent on them now that we just couldn't cope if they suddenly disappeared. And what about the incredible modes of transport we have? One hundred and fifty years ago, most people couldn't have imagined travelling by car. But today, just about everybody has one – and couldn't do without it. The idea of flying in an aircraft was the stuff of dreams just a century ago, but today it's a necessary reality. And by the looks of things, the geeks in technical laboratories are coming up with a million and one more gadgets that will all make life even faster and apparently easier in the future. I recently read that by 2050, a plane will be developed capable of flying from London to Sydney in around two hours. Wow – no more stopovers in Malaysia or Singapore. Think about it: a future generation will look back to today and wonder how we coped with flights that took more than 24 hours for the same journey.

The twenty-first century's emphasis on speed has led to an expectation that what we demand, we get. But the buy now, pay later culture has led to huge amounts of debt that are affecting the world economy. Patience is often a dirty word in our consumerist culture that wants everything as quickly and cheaply as possible.

Process

Of course, some miracles do happen instantly. For example, the man with leprosy whom Jesus met in Matthew 8:1–4 was 'immediately' healed as a result of Jesus' word. The man possessed by an evil spirit in Mark 1:21–28 was miraculously and instantly delivered at a simple command from Jesus. But while some miracles happen quickly, others take place over a period of time. Often, God requires a birthing process – otherwise it would prove all too much for us to handle in one go. Of course, the idea of some miracles not happening immediately will probably come as a shock to many Christians who are well and truly caught up in consumerism. However, there are many biblical examples of this being the case. One in particular takes precedence over them all. This miracle involved controversy, courage and choirs of angels.

Angelic Visitation

One day, the angel Gabriel visited a young woman called Mary. Life was going well for her. She was engaged to be married to Joseph. But in the midst of her preparations for marriage, she received some news that was shocking, startling and sensational, all at the same time. Gabriel announced to her that she was 'highly favoured' and chosen to bear a child who would be the Son of God. She asked, 'How will this be?' and the angel explained that the Holy Spirit would miraculously cause her to conceive.

What thoughts must Mary have pondered in her heart when she heard this? She must have asked herself some other questions, not least what would Joseph think about all this? After all, could he reasonably be expected to believe her when she tried to explain that she was pregnant, not by another man but as the result of an immaculate conception that was beyond her own control? But despite all the questions, Mary responded with faith and acceptance, saying to the angel, 'I am the Lord's servant. May it be to me as you have said.' The song she sang in Luke 1:46–55 gives us an insight into the measure of the woman, her love for God, her complete trust in his word and her utter dependence on his goodness. She sang, 'My soul glorifies the Lord and my spirit rejoices in God my Saviour.'

Just six months earlier, Zechariah, the husband of Mary's cousin Elizabeth, also had an angelic visitation from Gabriel. Elizabeth was barren and well on in years. However, the angel informed him that his wife would bear a son whose name was to be John (the Baptist). Since Elizabeth couldn't have children and was well beyond the age of childbearing anyway, Zechariah asked, 'How can I be sure of this? I am an old man and my wife is well on in years.' But Gabriel's response to this question was different: Zechariah was struck dumb until the day the child was born.

So what was the difference between Mary's questions and Zechariah's? Surely it was reasonable for both to ask what was on their hearts? The answer can be summed up in one word: trust. Mary's questioning didn't doubt what the angel said, but merely asked how the miracle would come about. Zechariah's query, however, was based on doubt: he was not convinced that what God had already ordained would actually happen. By striking him dumb, Gabriel was effectively silencing his unbelief. God does not mind us asking him questions, so long as they're asked in faith. It's when they're posed from a standpoint of cynicism that he has an issue.

Elizabeth went on to miraculously give birth to John, and a little later Mary gave birth to her son Jesus. Despite the poor conditions in which she gave birth, the hosts of heaven marvelled that night, with choirs of angelic beings singing, 'Glory to God in the highest , and on earth peace to men on whom his favour rests' (Luke 2:14). What a performance that must have been.

There are rich principles to be gleaned from looking at the miracle of Jesus' birth. The Son of God didn't just appear on earth as the saviour of the world. He went through a process. There was birth. There was childhood. There was adolescence. There was adulthood. There was maturity. There was death. And then there was resurrection. Charles Wesley's famous Christmas hymn 'Hark! The herald angels sing' focuses on the incarnation of Christ and contains a line that in my view is among the greatest he ever wrote: 'Veiled in flesh the Godhead see, hail the incarnate deity.'

There are lessons that we can learn from the miraculous birth and subsequent life of Jesus in our own quest to see more miracles. We shall now look at some of these.

1. There Is the Moment of Conception

The Spirit is the one who caused Mary to conceive. Before a miracle happens, there always has to be a Holy Spirit moment of conception. This may be brought on by a crisis. There are, after all, circumstances that we encounter in life where nothing other than a miracle is needed, perhaps an illness or a financial struggle. Other times, the conception of the miracle is sparked by a dream or vision for the future. Maybe God calls you to enter into a particular aspect of ministry but you look at your lack of resources and conclude that you need a miracle if the dream is ever to come about. So what will it take for you to make the vision happen? What steps do you need to take so that you can position yourself to experience the miracle?

Some pursue the wrong approach, which says, 'I'll wait until I have enough money and resources – then I'll begin to appropriate the thing that God has placed on my heart.' But this is not how Kingdom faith works. It's in your times of lack that you must sow as much seed as you have into the dream. That is really what the conception of a miracle is about – impregnating your vision with the seed of faith. Only then are you positioning yourself to see the impossible made possible.

When he was a young boy, Reinhard Bonnke had a vision to preach the Gospel to millions of people in Africa. But it took years of sowing in faith before the dream became a reality. Well over five decades later, he fulfilled a passion he'd had to communicate God's good news to more than one million people in a single service. This happened in Lagos, Nigeria. Many millions of people have been impacted with the Gospel because of the seed he has sown.

On a visit to Pakistan in 2007, I preached at a church with more than five thousand members. I asked the pastor what had led to that kind of growth. The answer I received was both humbling and mesmerizing. He told me he had had a dream twenty-five years before to establish something significant in the militant town where he was based. For the first five years, he and his wife sowed everything they had into the area and built up the congregation to around a thousand people. But the local community leaders became unhappy with the growth, and one day they gave him an ultimatum: either he left the area and closed down the church within twenty-four hours or he and his family would be killed. Twenty-four hours later, a small crowd carrying guns and knives arrived at his home. The pastor opened the door and invited the angry mob to come inside. They were amazed at what they found. You see, the night before, God had instructed him to 'bless those who curse you' by feeding his enemies. So he and his wife gathered everything they had in their little kitchen, presented it attractively and invited the men to eat with them. They accepted, and after a number of hours the community leaders said, 'We have never seen such an act of kindness. Because of this, you are welcome to stay in this town.' From then on he experienced many more miraculous moments on the way to even greater expansion, and a church today of five thousand – and growing.

For a miracle to happen, we often need to sow seeds of faith, even when the ground around us seems infertile. Sow with an attitude of expectancy, even when it doesn't seem to make much sense.

2. There Is the Process of Pregnancy

Even though Mary was told that she would give birth to the Son of God, she still had to go through nine months of pregnancy, just as any other woman would. But inside her was the Christ, developing, forming and dependent on the care of his carrier. This is a profound mystery, that the eternal Son of the living God should be carried in the womb of a human being. It tells us something about

God: he uses people to fulfil his purposes.

While some miracles are immediate, others need to be carried and developed over a period of time. When I launched out as an evangelist, I had (and still have) a vision to reach many people with the Gospel, to see football stadiums and large concert halls filled to capacity with thousands of people hearing the good news of Jesus Christ. But I wasn't very encouraged when sometimes I'd speak to congregations of as few as ten people. Yet even in those times when there was very little response, I knew in my heart that I was carrying something bigger. A significant vision was developing deep in my spirit. I understood that my current smallness was not destiny. Far from it: I was only too aware that as seemingly challenging as things were, they were crucial steps in the process of becoming the person God wanted me to be. The process of pregnancy can't be rushed and requires a lot of patience.

The most important thing you can do in the 'pregnancy' stage of a miracle is to maintain a healthy spiritual life. An unhealthy spirituality can actually damage and stunt the growth of what is taking place on the inside. God must always be our fulfilment. Paul spoke of our complete dependence of God in Acts 17:28, saying, 'In him we live and move and have our being.' Our expectation and hope must be firmly rooted in him.

3. There Is the Labour of Birth

Men really don't have much to complain of compared with what women have to go through in childbearing. After they've carried the baby for more than nine months the time comes to give birth. The labour is (I'm told) painful and uncomfortable, and can be long and protracted, sometimes lasting many hours. But when the baby is born, the agony and suffering are well and truly worth it, as a little miracle of life is introduced into the world.

In the process of giving birth to the miracle that has been conceived in your spirit, there will always be pressure. It's anything but glamorous and there is often little sympathy from others. Think about it: even though Mary was carrying the Son of God, there was still no room for her in the inn. Few seemed to realize the significance of who she was pregnant with. The only place available for the birth was an old barn. It's all too easy to view the stable scene with Christmas lights and tinsel. But nothing could be farther from reality. It would have been dirty, unhygienic and putrid with the smell of animal dung. It certainly wouldn't have passed any of today's health and safety regulations. But that's where Jesus was born.

It's a mistake to expect every miracle to come easily. This certainly wasn't the case with the birth of the Son of the living God. But after conception and the process of pregnancy, even after the struggles involved during the birth, there is nothing more exciting in the world than a miracle. God's timing is always right. And this was especially true of the birth of Jesus. Paul refers to this in Galatians 4:4, where he says, 'But when the time had fully come, God sent his Son, born of a woman, born under law.' Your miracle will happen when God's time for it 'fully' comes.

4. There Is the Tenderness of Infancy

I love Christmas time. Presents, family get-togethers and food all make for a fabulous Advent season, in my view.

And of course, don't forget the good old carols we all love to sing in the splendour of a candlelit church. But there's one Christmas hymn in particular that baffles me. I must admit that every time I sing 'Away in a manger', the words really do strike me as a bit unreal, especially 'The cattle are lowing, the baby awakes, but little Lord Jesus, no crying he makes.' This paints a warm, glowing picture of the baby Jesus, totally unperturbed by the noise of the animals in the stable: they have just woken him, but there is not a tear in the eye of this little one. Ahh – heart-melting stuff.

But it wasn't like that. Jesus cried. He needed to be looked after. He was an infant, dependent on his mother for protection and care. He needed food to eat and clothes to wear. Like all babies, he was hard work. But there is nothing more innocent than a newborn child, oblivious to the evils of this world. And there was plenty of trouble when Jesus was born. His very life was under threat. Herod knew that a significant child had been born, and as a precaution he ordered that every boy under the age of two be killed so that there would be no chance of this newborn 'king' posing a threat to his rule. But an angel had already given Joseph instructions to leave for Egypt (Matt. 2:13), and they stayed there until Herod died.

While the birth of a miracle is an undoubted blessing for the recipient, other people can feel insecure or threatened by it. The newly birthed miracle needs protection and care. The enemy of our souls knows better than anybody the power of its potential. There is often an attempt to kill the miracle in its infancy, before it has the opportunity to grow any more. For this reason, we have a responsibility to listen to what God is saying and be sensitive to his leading. This will help us keep the miracle safe from those who would wish to spoil it.

Miracles are tender at the stage of infancy, and they require us to have as much courage and conviction as at any other stage of their birth.

5. There Is the Misunderstanding of Youth

Jesus grew in wisdom and stature. Each year, he was taken to Jerusalem to celebrate the feast of the Passover. One year in particular, when Jesus was 12, he stayed behind in the temple when his parents set off for home. When they realized he wasn't with them, there was a desperate search to find him. Meanwhile, Jesus was happily conversing with the teachers of the law. Luke 2:47 says, 'Everyone who heard him was amazed at his understanding and his answers.' Eventually, Mary and Joseph found him and were 'astonished', not so much by his brilliance but because they thought he had been inconsiderate in not staying with them. But Jesus was no ordinary son – and they more than anyone should have known that. They misunderstood him when he tried to explain that he was in his 'Father's house' (Luke 2:49): after all, he was the Son of God.

After the birth of a miracle, as it moves on from infancy to maturity, there will often be misunderstanding, especially in the early stages. There are four types of people who you can expect to come across in your journey into the miraculous: the cautious, the concerned, the critical and the committed.

i. The cautious

These people are sometimes for you, sometimes against you. They simply observe the reaction of other people and then follow the crowd. In reality, such people make up the vast majority you come across in your journey into the miraculous. We should never depend too much on the cautious when they follow us, because their support can be fickle. This is classically illustrated in Jesus' later ministry. One week, the crowd shouted, 'Blessed is he who comes in the name of the Lord.' The next, they cried, 'Crucify him!'

ii. The concerned

People in this category genuinely believe they have your best interests at heart, but they are sincerely wrong. When you begin to sow in faith towards the miracle you believe for, they express concern that you are doing the wrong thing, not convinced that the miracle could ever happen in the first place. Love people like this – but don't spend too much time listening to them. They just haven't got it.

iii. The critical

These people are largely motivated by their own self-interest. Their attitude is akin to that of the Pharisees in the Bible. The Pharisees resented the fact that Jesus seemed to be more popular than they were. When he healed the blind man in John 9, they tried to undermine the miracle by suggesting that such a thing could not happen on the Sabbath. After Lazarus was raised from the dead, their hatred of Jesus grew even more venomous and they plotted his death. You will always have critics as you journey into the miraculous. But don't let them sidetrack you. Just stay focused on God.

iv. The committed

These are the most important people in your life. Jesus had people like this around him – and so should you.

They believe in you. They understand your heart. When the committed ask you difficult questions, you know they're not doing it out of spite but because they want to see you experience even greater miracles.

When you experience misunderstanding, just keep pressing on. You will get there.

6. There Is the Coming of Adulthood

This is the final stage of a miracle. When Jesus was 30 years old, his ministry began in earnest. He had grown up. The little baby was now a fully grown man. Mary and Joseph had to let him go. He had a divine mandate to fulfil. His time had come. Interestingly, his ministry only lasted around three-and-a-half years. But what a difference he made.

There comes a moment in the life of any miracle when we have to be willing to let go. Many people try to hold on as long as possible, but reluctance to release it can prove an obstacle to future progress. How many great churches have been devastated by leadership that just wouldn't let go? Many a powerful ministry ended prematurely because it was smothered by leaders who didn't know how to release it to the next generation.

It's impossible to imagine what it was like for Mary as she watched the son she had borne standing condemned for crimes he had never committed. She's the one who nursed him, fed him, looked after him and raised him as a boy. What agony she must have gone through as she saw her beautiful son being crucified. Words could not express the emotional pain she suffered. But as heartbreaking as the crucifixion was for her, it seems she knew deep down that it was utterly necessary, as this was the only way Jesus could reconcile people to God. It was this very act that was making possible the greatest miracle in the whole world – that people could have their sin forgiven and receive everlasting life. But it came at a terrible cost.

Death made way for burial. But burial had to make way for resurrection. Only by dying and rising again could Jesus defeat the power of sin and death. This was an eternal investment on Jesus' part, the wounds and scars of his suffering being reminders of the price he had paid for humanity. How great is our God.

The Long-Haul Approach

In our pursuit of the miraculous, we would be wise to remember the principles of Jesus' birth and life. Instant results are not always guaranteed in our quest to see the supernatural. Instead, it's a journey, and it sometimes involves the long-haul approach. It's like the difference between a sprint and a marathon. Sprinting is an intense but short period of running, say over 100 metres. A marathon, however, takes much longer and requires a slower pace. Undoubtedly, some miracles are like 100-metre sprints, happening quickly, even suddenly. However, the fulfilment of God-given visions and dreams is invariably more like a marathon. This is why Hebrews 12:1 encourages us to 'run with perseverance the race marked out for us'. It's an altogether longer process that needs persistence and longevity, like the process of birthing a miracle. But the goal is worth the journey. Remember, at every stage along the way, trust is needed, not merely in results but in who God is.

10

MIRACLES ON THE MENU

There are more than thirty-one thousand of them all over the globe. On any major highway, you're never too far from one. The logo is instantly recognisable, even from a distance. It's a hugely successful multi-billion-dollar industry. Mums adore it. Dads admire it. Kids devour it. As the company's own strap line says, 'I'm lovin' it.' Yes, it's official: everybody loves McDonald's. Well, everyone except me. I hate it.

But why, you may wonder, should I detest such a successful brand enjoyed by millions of people the world over? Is it because I'm a posh snob who refuses to consume the food of the common people? Or is it anything to do with the fact that I always feel hungry again within thirty minutes of eating one? Or maybe my reasons are political: am I a frustrated lefty who despises the capitalism of which McDonald's is the absolute epitome?

Well, here's why I actually detest McDonald's. It's boring. It's bland. It's, it's yellow.

My wife and I were recently on holiday in Paris. After dropping the luggage off at our hotel room, we decided we'd go out and get some food as we hadn't eaten anything since breakfast. We strolled along the classy

Parisian streets on that beautiful spring evening, and not long into our walk we came by a McDonald's restaurant. At first (and for the merest split second), we thought about going in to grab a quick Mcbite to eat. But hungry as I was, I really couldn't bring myself to do it. Why, I thought, should we restrict ourselves to a corporate menu of dull processed food when we're in Paris, the good-food capital of the world? So we continued on in the hope of finding another eating place that was still open.

Our patience was duly rewarded when we eventually found the most wonderful restaurant which served delicious home-cooked meals. That evening, we dined on frog's legs and snails for starters, followed by finely cooked Beef Crêpe Maison served with an array of seasoned vegetables. Then for dessert we had *contraste chocopassionnément* – irresistible warm chocolate mousse with passion fruit sorbet that made the mouth water and the heart beat a little faster. There simply was no comparison between the authentic French food and a Big Mac and fries.

Predictability

Sometimes I wonder if McDonald's is the role model for many churches. Every week without fail, the same menu of bland spirituality is served up, largely unchanged, monotonous and lacking in variety. Surely this is not what church was ever meant to be? Where do miracles feature on the menu of most churches? Where is the power of God? Often no space or opportunity is given to God for him to do what only he can do. Instead, set programmes have been turned into today's speciality. Overdependence on gimmickry, technology and Power

Point presentations has negated the need for prayer, devotion and the word of the Lord. The only real faith that's on display in many churches is in the power of electricity, and if that doesn't work, there's trouble!

Ten-point sermons are what many preachers are dishing out. But never mind Power Point presentations – where's the power of the Holy Spirit? Where's the prophetic? Where's the excitement of the supernatural? Even postmodern people now question the relevance of predictability.

You see, predictability can at times be a friend. But more often than not, it's an enemy. It stifles creativity and smothers individuality. And this is especially true of church.

For example, early in the twentieth century an African-American preacher called William J. Seymour encouraged people in his church not just to understand the Bible in their heads, but to enter into an experience of the power of the Holy Spirit for themselves. However, his denominational overseers disliked this, since it wasn't the norm, so much so that they removed him from the church where he was pastor. Seymour relocated to Los Angeles and found a derelict old building on Azusa Street, where he hosted meetings to which anyone who wanted to experience the miraculous could come. Many did. But Seymour was the subject of much ridicule from other church leaders who saw him as a dangerous and blatant threat to their churches. There were numerous attempts to undermine him, but none of them succeeded. Today, it is widely accepted that the events of Azusa Street were the birth of modern Pentecostalism, with Seymour celebrated as a founding father.

Smith Wigglesworth was another man who moved in the miraculous and saw many incredible healings as a result of his ministry. In his day, he was largely dismissed as a maverick, avoided by many church leaders because of his controversial methods of praying for people. Yet now, he's celebrated as a hero of the faith. His books are a multi-million-dollar industry. So why do people love him today? It's simple: he's dead. No one is threatened by him any more, because stories of his ministry can be read from the comfort of a living room, without directly affecting the reader.

This basically sums up why so many churches follow the McDonald's formula each week. It's to do with a lack of real adventure, and being unwilling to have a bit of flexibility and courage to change what's on the current menu. Sure, they can devour all the latest books on leadership and even attend conferences on how to make church successful. But deep down, their only real appetite is for predictability: they're fearful and even threatened by anything on offer that's different from the 'norm'. Their taste buds are never really challenged – they prefer instead to feed off the same restrictive choice of spiritual food and subject others to the same.

But the Holy Spirit is the master connoisseur. He's never predictable. In fact, he's like the wind – always moving. Surely if he were given free rein in church, things would be very different. Predictability would no longer be the main course. Instead, fresh revelation would be the order of the day – and blandness would become unpalatable. It would be like moving from a sub-standard café to the finest of restaurants. There just isn't any comparison.

Released into the Prophetic

When I first started to preach as an evangelist, I used to depend very heavily on sermon notes. I would write reams of A4 pages, sometimes as many as twenty sheets. Then when I stood up to preach, I would feel secure in the knowledge that I had my notes to keep me on track. But all that changed one night.

I was speaking at a students' conference in the city of Bangalore. The venue was a large room without windows. The meeting that night had been quite electrifying, with a very real sense of God's presence. I eventually stood up to preach and everything went very well for the first twenty minutes. But in a moment, the situation became completely different. As I was in full flow, there was a sudden power cut. The P.A. system switched off, and worst of all, the room was in pitch-black darkness. This of course meant that I couldn't see my notes. Since the people were used to regular power surges, they simply remained in their seats and expected me to keep preaching. But I had a problem: I relied so heavily on my notes, I really didn't know what to do without them.

I turned to my interpreter, who was standing next to me on the platform. I said, 'What should I do now?' He replied clinically, 'Just keep preaching.' In shock, I tried to explain that I couldn't continue without being able to see my notes. I hoped he might help me out, but he just stood there in exactly the same pose and repeated his previous words: 'Just keep preaching.'

This was a dilemma for me. My overdependence on the security of sermon notes meant that I was not ready for the unexpected. As I stood on the platform in front of nearly a thousand students, all wondering what I was doing, I cried out to God in my heart, 'Lord, help me! I really need you!' Quietly, in my spirit, I felt I heard God speak to me, saying, 'Tell the people, light must always overcome darkness.' The irony of that statement wasn't lost on me – but I thought I'd better speak it out and see what happened. With a quiet voice, I said, 'Light always overcomes darkness.' My interpreter immediately translated this and the response was a resounding 'Amen' from the students. I said it again, this time with a slightly louder voice: 'Light must always overcome darkness.' This was again translated – and the students began to clap their hands and cheer. I remember thinking this one-line sermon had the potential to be the best I'd ever preached. As I said it a third time, suddenly it was as if the glory of God descended in that room. It was tangible. In the midst of it, the lights did come back on again. But now, having electricity didn't really matter too much any more. I was freed from the bondage of heavy reliance on sermon notes – and that night, I experienced a prophetic release that I'd never known before. To this day, I still get emails from students who were in that conference and remember words from God that were spoken over their lives. It was a truly unforgettable night – and one that changed my life for ever.

Change the Old Menu

Where is our faith rooted? In church there can be a tendency to trust more in what we've always done than in what God wants to do. The idea of not *feeling* in control is a step too far for many church leaders. Chefs are notoriously insecure and sensitive, many being reluctant to serve up anything that's not tried and tested for fear of how their customers might react if they don't like it. But when miracles are on the menu of church, they must always be accompanied with a generous serving of faith. It's as if God must now be appointed head chef and his instructions need to be followed. After all, isn't Jesus the head of the church?

And the truth is, whatever is currently going on, at some point down the line there will always be a need for a miracle. It may be to do with healing, finances, relationships or something completely unexpected – and the need normally comes out of the blue. Of course, some are able to rise to the challenge and experience a breakthrough. Sadly, however, many are caught out, unable to cope because what is needed is nothing short of a miracle, and this is something for which many churches simply can't cater.

The early church in the book of Acts certainly had miracles on the menu. Even in the midst of persecution, there was a sense of incredible excitement at the thought that anything could happen at any given moment. In Acts 3, Peter and John passed by a beggar who was lame from birth. He asked them for money but got a lot more than he bargained for. Peter's response was full of faith and authority: 'Silver or gold I do not have, but what I have I give you. In the name of Jesus Christ of Nazareth, walk' (Acts 3:6). Peter helped the man to his feet – and strength came into his legs and ankles so that he could walk, run and jump for the first time in his life. As a result of this miracle, Peter had the opportunity to preach to a huge crowd of onlookers – and five thousand of them gave their lives to Jesus Christ.

There must have been a real infectiousness about the early church. Word of the miracles performed by the apostles spread like wildfire. In Acts 5:15, it is recorded that people 'brought the sick into the streets and laid them on beds and mats' so that they could have the opportunity of being healed. Today, we'd class that as revival. But for them, it was normal.

Some 27 per cent of the book of Acts is devoted to extraordinary and charismatic activity. Here are four key ingredients that caused the early church to grow at a phenomenal rate, from which today's church could learn.

1. The excitement of the spontaneous

Church meetings in those early days could not be accused of being boring and uneventful. For example, in Acts 10, the Holy Spirit interrupted Peter's anointed sermon and filled everyone present, including the Gentiles. Then in Acts 12, as the church gathered to pray for Peter, who was in prison, he miraculously escaped with angelic assistance and returned to where the meeting was taking place. There was such jubilation at his release that they even forgot to let him into the building (Acts 12:14–15). In Acts 20:7–12, one man fell asleep during Paul's sermon and unfortunately fell from a three-storey building and died. But Paul rushed out and saw to it that he was raised from the dead. Eventful? You'd better believe it!

2. A release of the supernatural

There were prophetic visions, such as Saul's in Acts 9 which led to his conversion. At the same time, a man of God called Ananias also saw a vision in which God revealed exactly where Saul was and what had happened to him. Then there was Peter's vision in Acts 10, in which God revealed his purpose for the Gentiles. Supernatural activity was common in the life of the early church.

3. Large doses of signs and wonders

Philip the evangelist moved powerfully in the miraculous in Acts 8, and the result was that people 'paid close attention to what he said' (8:6). On another occasion, Paul was bitten by a venomous snake that 'fastened itself on his hand' (Acts 28:3–6). But far from being harmed, he miraculously suffered no ill effects at all. Such things stirred people to see something different about this new Christian community.

4. Great sensitivity to the voice of God

For example, Philip the evangelist was obedient to the instruction of an angel who told him to leave Samaria, where he was preaching to huge crowds, and go to the desert instead. While there, he only spoke to one man. But the Ethiopian eunuch, a treasury minister in the Queen's government, committed his life to Christ, and as a Christian, would now have the opportunity to influence people in high places with the message of Jesus. In Acts 16:6–10, Paul had the sensitivity to know that God was directing him to preach in the region of Macedonia through a vision he'd seen.

These ingredients (and more) led to amazing miracles. If the early church had not experienced these miracles, they would have been in serious trouble – and there would never have been the kind of growth they experienced. Miracles weren't abnormal, they were the norm. And so it ought to be the case today. But for this to happen, ingredients will need to change, some being added and others being taken out.

The Good Old Days

For those churches which are 'Pentecostal' or 'Charismatic' in flavour, there can also be a great danger, which is summed up in one word: 'sentimentalism'. It can be all too easy to become complacent, living off previous experiences of the miraculous – and considering those to be sufficient for today. But God has so much more for us to see.

In Isaiah 43:16–19, there is an interesting paradox. In one sentence, God reminds his people of past miracles. He tells them to remember that he is the one 'who made a way through the sea, a path through the mighty waters'. This is a reference to the astonishing miracle of deliverance that saved the children of Israel from being slaughtered by the army of Egypt. Yet in the next sentence, God tells his people, 'Forget the former things; do not dwell on the past. See, I am doing a new thing.' Is God suggesting that people should forget his past goodness? Far from it. It's actually a warning against sentimentality, living on the memories of the good old days. God now tells his people, 'I am making a way in the desert and streams in the wasteland.' The God who created dry in the midst of wet is the same God who can form wet in the midst of dry. There are miracles that are yet to be experienced.

Do or Die

When I was on ministry in India a few years ago, the church leaders I worked with were excited to tell me about one young evangelist whom God was using prolifically in the miraculous. He was fearless in his travels to various villages where the Gospel had never been heard. In one village, he began to preach on the street and a crowd gathered around him to hear what he was saying. He said, 'My God can save you,' and they listened. He declared, 'My God can forgive you,' and the people continued to hear him. Then he said, 'My God can even heal you.' However, when he said this, there was some disruption at the back of the 300-strong crowd. Suddenly, he noticed a woman pushing a man forward in an old-fashioned wheelchair. These were the elders of the village, very influential people. The woman stopped the young preacher in mid-flow and questioned him. 'You just said that your God can heal people. So today, if your God heals my husband, who has been unable to walk for many years, we will worship him as the only God. However, if he doesn't get healed, we will kill you.' Not exactly faith-inspiring, don't you think?

So the preacher was now in a serious predicament. Either God showed up – or he was dead. It was as stark as that. He went over to the man in the wheelchair, and simply quoted the words of Peter and John in Acts 3, 'Silver or gold I do not have, but what I have I give you. In the name of Jesus Christ of Nazareth, walk.' He then helped the man out of the wheelchair – and amazingly, he began to walk for the first time in many years. After this, the preacher finished off his street sermon and made an appeal for those who would like to worship Jesus as the only true and living God to come forward. Literally everyone who heard him (including the man who had been healed and his wife) gave their lives to Jesus that day.

Where Are the Miracles?

Someone once observed that if the Holy Spirit were taken out of the western church, 98 per cent of what it does would remain the same. That's a strong statement. But the point does have some validity. Many Christians have got used to a diet of convenience and spiritual junk food that often does more harm than good. They think this is as good as it gets – never having tasted what good spiritual food is really like.

The picture of Jesus knocking on the door of the Laodicean church in Revelation 3:20 is nothing short of tragic. What was it that reduced Christ to standing outside his own church, seeking entrance? What could possibly have led to this? It was all about that church's self-sufficiency and self-dependence. They felt they didn't need Jesus inside any more, as they had everything they needed. Of course, they wouldn't have verbalized those thoughts – but in their hearts that's what they really believed. They had developed an arrogant attitude that they could go it alone. How wrong they were. They didn't realize how bereft they were. Jesus said they were 'wretched, pitiful, poor, blind and naked'. And as if that were not bad enough, what was worse is that they didn't even know it.

The comparison between the church at Laodicea and the twenty-first-century western church is all too close for comfort. Interestingly though, Jesus didn't give up hope. He promised that if anyone opened the door, he would be more than happy to come and 'eat with him, and he with me'. The menu that Christ offers is not unhealthy and harmful, but full of only the very best ingredients.

Dependence

Moving in the miraculous really does require a new willingness to have complete dependence on God. Basic things like proactive prayer and a belief in the power of God's word take precedence over everything else. After all, if God doesn't show up, what's the point? Or as Moses put it in Exodus 33:15, 'If your Presence does not go with us, do not send us.'

The world doesn't need a corporately branded McChurch. Authenticity is what unchurched people are really searching for. That's not just about defining the doctrines of what we believe, but showing why we believe them through the way we live. Remember, in our visual society, people tend to see what they like before they like what they see. The blunt truth is that church doesn't grab people's attention. It's not distinctive enough. It doesn't really look very appetizing. And it should be. After all, the Gospel is the most incredible message in the whole universe. And that crucial dynamic of the miraculous is an intrinsic part of God's good news.

Why, then, can such a radical message be presented so clinically and unpalatably? How in the wide world has the Gospel been turned into a mundane monologue, plated up with a few songs and a quick prayer? It's a travesty. From beyond the grave, the words of Gandhi still provide food for thought. He said, 'You Christians look after a document containing enough dynamite to blow all civilization to pieces, turn the world upside down and bring peace to a battle-torn planet. But you treat it as though it is nothing more than a piece of literature.'

Well, that settles it. I've made my decision. I'm not going to follow the McDonald's formula for successful Christian leadership. I'm going with the Holy Spirit instead. It's scary sometimes, no doubt about it. But better to experience a little fear and at least get somewhere than remain in the comfort zone and go nowhere. Better to taste and see that the Lord is good than to stick to the old weary menu that's remained unchanged for far too long in so many churches.

It's time for a change in the offering. The old one has been too restricted for too long. In a world that is in desperate need of healing, we have the answers. Yet all too often there's a deafening silence from the church.

11

KEEP ON KEEPING ON

The best way to help others experience the miraculous is to have some personal experiences of your own that you can refer to. While it's important to study theology and glean a better understanding of the Bible, what you learn only becomes truly effective when you put it into practice. And it will always be a practice, in the same way that someone who studies medicine for years eventually practises as a doctor – or a student who graduates from law school goes on to practise as a lawyer. So in a sense we must continually be practitioners of the miraculous.

Of course, our personal experience of seeing miracles usually happens in the midst of times of need, even crisis. There is no easy route to take, but the more challenging the circumstance, the more credit God gets when he works the miracle through it.

Miracles in a Time of Need

When I started out as an evangelist, everything was going so well for me. Even though there wasn't much money coming in, I seemed to get by. Ministry was progressing, doors were opening, lots of people were becoming Christians at events where I spoke and miracles were occurring regularly. But then, everything started to go wrong. Have you ever noticed that problems are like buses – they all seem to come along at once.

I was involved in a car crash from which I miraculously escaped without so much as a scratch on my body. Then I became slightly ill – just a minor thing, but it lasted a period of months. Then to top it all off, I ran out of money. My home at the time was a little terraced house. My neighbour to the left was a well-known drug dealer in the area, and the neighbour to my right was a convicted criminal. Then there was me in the middle – Mr Evangelist. Good place for a guy like me to live, right? Well, I certainly didn't think so at the time. I really didn't like it.

One night in the midst of all this, I sat in my living room feeling that I'd taken as much as I could. So I made up my mind that I was going to quit the ministry. It wasn't that I was about to backslide and renounce my faith. No way. I loved God with all my heart. But I was so discouraged by the hassle of life, the lack of finances and the scarcity of resources that I felt it was too difficult to continue.

I had barely made up my mind when suddenly the Holy Spirit reminded me of a commitment I had made in my teens back in Belfast. You see, when I was 16, I said to God one day, 'Lord, whatever you want me to do, I will do it and be committed to it. Wherever you send me, I will go.' At the time, it felt like a really spiritual prayer, but little did I know then just how dangerous it really was. Now, as I sat in my little home in the midst of what for me was a crisis, it was as if the Holy Spirit was challenging me, 'Now I want you to live that prayer.' This really wasn't what I wanted to listen to.

Often we ask God to speak to us, but the problem is that he doesn't always say what we want to hear. Instead, he tells us what we *need* to listen to. That night, even though I had already made up my mind to quit, I knew that wasn't what God desired. He actually wanted me to stick with it. So that's what I did. Was it easy? No it wasn't. But it was during that time of keeping on with it that I learned to experience the miraculous for myself. Some days I'd turn up at my home, and groceries would be sitting at the door. Bearing in mind that I told no one about my need, to this day I'm not sure where they came from. Perhaps they were delivered by angels. Who knows? But life was still tough. The financial situation was not getting any better: each month it was a real struggle to pay the bills and have enough to live on at the end.

Out of Petrol

One day, I received a phone call from a church that was well over 100 miles from where I lived. The pastor asked me if I would go there to preach at relatively short notice, in a few days' time. So I agreed. A few days later, I got into my car and went to turn the engine on, ready to travel to the church. But to my surprise, a little orange light started flashing at the bottom of the dashboard, telling me there was only a small amount of petrol in the tank. I was flabbergasted. I got out of the car and asked God a question that many Christians have asked at some point in their lives: 'Lord, why me? Why am I going through this?' It seemed so unfair. There I was, a servant of God, and I didn't even have enough money to fill the tank with petrol. It was totally demoralizing. But then, I felt the Holy Spirit whisper to me, 'Get into your car and drive.' Well, that had to be God speaking, because I certainly wouldn't have told myself to do such a seemingly ridiculous thing. Driving without petrol: pretty crazy, don't you think?

I got back into the car and switched the engine on. I remember thinking, 'This has to be the stupidest thing I've ever done in my entire life. But here goes anyway.' So I began to drive, expecting the car to conk out at any moment. Eventually I covered ten miles, amazed I'd even got that far. Then I got to twenty miles, and thirty miles, even up to forty miles. At this point, I remember being unable to control my hands as they were shaking so badly. But at around the halfway point, a strange thing happened. An inexplicable peace entered my heart. Somehow I knew that everything was going to be just fine. My hands were no longer shaking. I should have been concerned, but I wasn't. I even became a bit worried that I wasn't worried.

I continued on – sixty miles, seventy miles, eighty miles, ninety miles, a hundred miles – until I eventually pulled up on the hilly road (facing downwards) beside the church where I was to be the preacher. I just sat there for a few moments. I decided I wouldn't tell anyone about this, as I didn't think anyone would believe me.

The meeting was quite incredible that night. Everyone was very conscious of the presence of God. I preached, and afterwards people gave their lives to Christ. Then I prayed for people to be healed, and some fabulous stories emerged.

At the end of the meeting, I prayed quietly to the Lord, 'Thank you for getting me here tonight. It really has been incredible. However, there's just one issue – I've got to get home again.'

Not having told anyone about my need, I stood at the exit as people left the church, shaking them by the hand, and looking everybody straight in the eye as if to say,

'Might you have a word from God for me?' So many people said, 'That was fantastic tonight' or, 'Keep up the good work.' One man even said, 'Let me give you a quick piece of advice, young man. Stay humble and God will use you even more in the future,' after which he winked at me, and then left. In my mind I thought, 'If only you knew, mister!'

The auditorium eventually emptied until there were just three people left: the pastor, an elder and a little old lady. To be honest, my heart was not filled with too much hope. I went over to them to say goodbye. The elder said to me, 'We have an honorarium for you, but we'll have to send it by post. Hope you don't mind.' I just faked a smile and with a slightly higher pitched voice than normal said, 'That's fine' – yet inwardly thinking, 'Help!'

I said my goodbyes and was nearly out of the exit when suddenly the little old lady shouted after me, 'Yoohoo! Don't leave yet – I want a word with you.' I stopped and turned round as she walked towards me. I noticed that she had a small brown envelope in her hand – and she instantly had my attention. The lady explained, 'This afternoon as I was praying, I felt the Lord speak to me and tell me to bless the servant of God who preaches tonight,' at which point she lifted up the envelope and gave it to me. With great dignity and elegance, I graciously accepted the lady's gift and thanked her for it. Once I was out of the building, I lost all my composure and ripped the envelope open as quickly as possible. Inside, there was a cash gift – well in excess of any money I needed for petrol to get home. Since the petrol station was next door to the church, I rolled the car down the hill and right to the pump, where I filled the tank to the brim.

On the drive home, I remember feeling exhausted, having gone through such a mix of emotions. But a thought occurred to me. What would have happened if I'd stayed at home instead and merely blamed God, asking, 'Why am I going through this?' The answer struck me – absolutely nothing would have happened. I would never have experienced a miracle. Sometimes, what we see as our greatest need is really just a miracle in disguise. It's a matter of having the audacity to trust God – even when it doesn't seem anything is going right. I learned more about the miraculous in that one experience than I ever could have done in three years of theological study.

The Journey Goes On

And so the journey of ministry went on. Having spent four years working as the full-time salaried evangelist for a network of churches in the north of England, I felt it was time to move on and take up the national and international opportunities that were coming my way. Without a penny in the bank, I launched out again. The truth is I had no idea how I would live from month to month without a regular salary. But God gave me supernatural wisdom and a large dose of faith to accompany it. I launched a charitable trust called Global Harvest that would facilitate the aims of my ministry: reaching the unchurched, releasing evangelists and resourcing the church.

Without any big finance campaigns or pleas for support, people came to me, saying, 'We want to get behind you – how can we?' Then a number of churches that I have always enjoyed a great relationship with got behind me – and within a relatively short space of time regular support was coming in, so that I didn't have to scrape by for a living. It really did prove to me that when you step out in faith, having heard from God, you really can expect God to miraculously provide. It doesn't always come when you want it, though. Sometimes God leaves it to the last possible moment before he meets your need. Why is that? Well, for a start, it would be no fun if it didn't happen like that. But in the end, God is looking for faith that will believe to the very end. Perhaps that explains why.

Life here on earth is surely just one big learning curve. But so often we are reluctant to relish the new, preferring instead to live off the old. The desire for the familiar often defeats the possibilities of a new day. A lack of hunger to learn more leads to apathy and acceptance of the status quo. But people who move in faith don't live like that. There's never a dull moment in the life of a true practitioner of the miraculous. Every new experience demands trust. Each fresh challenge requires courage to journey on. Without a willingness to relish and embrace change, we will never discover more of God's glory and explore deeper realms of his wonder.

Here are eight helpful pointers to inspire you to keep on keeping on in your journey to see more of the miraculous.

1. Prepare for the adventure of your life

Christopher Columbus was a passionate explorer. He relished the journey as much as the destination. Someone once said of him, 'He left Europe but he didn't know where he was going. He got there but didn't know where he was. He came back again but he didn't know where he'd been.' But Columbus enjoyed the journey so much that he did it three times in seven years, and in the process, he discovered the new world (i.e. the Americas).

On your journey towards each new miracle, be ready to learn something different about God, yourself and life. Be willing to have your horizons widened and your perspective challenged. On your way, you'll be stretched as well as inspired. But every step is one of faith, towards becoming the person God wants you to be. Remember that we don't walk merely by physical sight but with our trust in the one who knows and sees the way ahead. Miracles happen when God reveals what we haven't yet seen with our eyes and we then trust him to see it through.

2. *Be willing to embrace new challenges*

Caleb was 85 years old. He had already been a warrior for at least half his life. Yet retirement was the last thing on his mind. He felt fresher and stronger than ever (Josh. 14:11) and was ready to fight another battle en route to the promised land. What an inspiration.

Whatever God has promised you for your life, one thing is for sure – he never guarantees an easy ride. We will always encounter new challenges. Some choose to give up, opting for an easier life instead. But Caleb's old comrade Joshua refused that, saying, 'As for me and my household, we will serve the LORD' (Josh. 24:15).

Experiencing the miraculous will require a willingness to embrace each new circumstance that we encounter. Don't be overawed by the bigness of what's before you. Instead, be inspired by the magnificence of who is for you. He's the God of miracles – and he will not let you down.

3. *Listen most to those who journey with you*

Everybody has an opinion. That's why it's unwise to listen to too many people. The mix of views will only bring confusion and instability, and won't help you on your way. Be gracious when people express their perspective, but make sure you listen most to those who consistently journey with you. This is something I have learned the hard way in my ministry. In my desire to be accountable and transparent, I allowed people to speak into my life who I should not have. They neither knew me nor understood where I was going, bringing ideas that they genuinely thought were helpful but frankly were anything but.

Those who journey with you will not always agree with you. But a true friend is marked by honesty, encouraging you when you do well and pointing out where you could do better. We all need people like this in our quest to see more of the miraculous.

4. Don't get sidetracked by the wrong issues

In Acts 1:6, the disciples asked Jesus one final question before his ascension: 'Lord, are you at this time going to restore the kingdom to Israel?' It sounded reasonable enough – but it was totally inappropriate at that moment. Jesus replied, 'It is not for you to know the times or dates the Father has set by his own authority.' He then went on to talk about the power and purpose of the Spirit's work through them – reminding them that they were in effect going to change the whole world very shortly.

We can so easily lose sight of the big picture by focusing on side issues instead. In journeying to see more of the miraculous, we ought to do what someone once said and 'keep the main thing the main thing'. Distraction is one of the biggest tools of the enemy. He wants us to miss our miracle moment for the sake of focusing on something that God already has under control anyway.

Don't get sidetracked. Stay focused. Your miracle is coming.

5. Remain fresh and positive

How is it possible to stay fresh and positive on your way to seeing more of the miraculous? It's all about having total reliance on the one who is leading you, Jesus. Takes the pressure off, don't you think? In John 15, he says he is the vine and we are the branches. The only way the branches can remain strong and healthy is if they constantly feed off the source.

Psalm 23 paints an amazing picture of the good shepherd (God) leading the sheep (his people). 'He makes me lie down in green pastures, he leads me beside quiet waters.'

We so often carry stress that was never meant to be ours to bear. In moments of crisis when we desperately need a miracle, one of the lessons God wants us to learn is the secret of rest. It's a matter of trusting him – and if there's real faith going on, why should we be stressed? Why should we worry? After all, Jesus said, 'My yoke is easy and my burden is light' (Matt. 11:30).

6. Remember, you've got nothing to prove

The only people who have anything to prove in life are those who are insecure. They're desperate to let everybody know what they can achieve, often motivated by a desire to prove their detractors wrong (whoever they may be). But the Christian life is not about proving anything. It's simply about seeing and recognizing God for who he is. He, after all, is the one who sits on the throne. There's no threat to his rule. It's not that we need to 'make God famous'. That's already well and truly the case. The purpose of the church is to help people experience their own personal relationship with Jesus.

Our journey towards the miraculous is one on which we develop greater confidence in God and his word. Our security is firmly rooted in Jesus Christ. Jesus himself didn't perform miracles at Herod's request, because he was not interested in entertaining anybody (Luke 23:8). He didn't need to – and he still doesn't. God is God whether we see his miracles or not. In the midst of Moses' excuses about why he felt unable to fulfil his purpose, God reminded him, 'I am who I am.' This is where our confidence ought to rest.

7. *Enjoy every experience*

Enjoy the good times and the not-so-good times too. The latter sounds a bit ridiculous, doesn't it? But it is possible. In Acts 5, the apostles witnessed incredible miracles as they laid their hands on people on the streets. But when the religious establishment brought them to court shortly afterwards for preaching about Jesus, they were beaten and flogged. However, instead of getting angry and bitter at something so harsh and unjust, they left 'rejoicing because they had been counted worthy of suffering disgrace for the Name' (Acts 5:41).

In Acts 16 Paul and Silas, in prison after being falsely accused by an angry slave trader whose servant had been miraculously loosed from demonic possession, prayed and sang songs of praise to God at midnight. Even when an earthquake struck (coincidentally?) they didn't bother to escape, though they could have. As a result, the jailkeeper saw something different about them – and received the greatest miracle of all, eternal life.

Enjoy the journey, bumps and all. Be an inspiration to others.

8. Sow today for what you believe will happen tomorrow

Alfred Nobel, inventor of the basic components of dynamite, was an incredibly rich man who had everything he could have wanted or needed in life. But shortly after the death of his brother, while reading a daily newspaper he was shocked to come across his own obituary. A journalist had mistakenly been informed that Alfred, not his brother, had died. Nobel was horrified by what he read. The gist of the column was that he would be remembered as a man who had contributed to war and instability, since he had sold his new invention to many countries.

That day, Alfred Nobel decided he would redefine his own legacy. He wanted to be remembered as a man of peace, not of war. So he sowed much of his wealth into projects that contributed to and promoted peace in the world, establishing the Nobel Peace Prize. Today, the name Nobel will for ever be associated with peace. All because he sowed into his legacy and decided to make a positive difference.

The life you live today is a prophecy of what your legacy will be tomorrow. Believing for miracles is not just a matter of hoping that someday a great 'revival' will come – even though that could happen. There's got to be more to it than that. You've got to sow in faith. That involves time, finance, talent and effort. But the harvest is always worth it.

Finish Well

The day of miracles is not over. This is a message that the church needs to hear again and again. In a world where people's hopes and dreams sit alongside their fears and concerns, it would be a mistake for Christians merely to engage in endless theological arguments, debates and discussion papers. Frankly, there isn't time for that. The hour is urgent. The call is desperate. Yet the answer is closer than we often realize. It's in the heart of every believer in Jesus Christ. We need as never before to rise up in the power of the Holy Spirit, with a renewed passion and conviction to communicate God's message of good news and see it accompanied by signs and wonders. Miracles are not an optional extra to the Gospel – they are an intrinsic part of the message.

Paul's concluding remarks to the Christians at Rome included this: 'Therefore I glory in Christ Jesus in my service to God. I will not venture to speak of anything except what Christ has accomplished through me in leading the Gentiles to obey God by what I have said and done – by the power of signs and miracles, through the power of the Spirit. So from Jerusalem all the way around to Illyricum, I have fully proclaimed the gospel of Christ' (Rom. 15:17–19).

As we engage in the ultimate mission of reaching lost people, let's move on with faith and confidence, determined that one day we'll look back and, like the apostle Paul, declare that we too 'fully proclaimed the gospel of Christ'. The best is yet to come.